STUDIES IN ENGLISH LITERATURES

Edited by Koray Melikoğlu

Thomas F. Halloran

James Joyce
Developing Irish Identity

A Study of the Development
of Postcolonial Irish Identity in the Novels
of James Joyce

STUDIES IN ENGLISH LITERATURES

Edited by Koray Melikoğlu

ISSN 1614-4651

2   *Paul Fox (ed.)*
    Decadences
    Morality and Aesthetics in British Literature
    ISBN 3-89821-573-3

3   *Daniel M. Shea*
    James Joyce and the Mythology of Modernism
    ISBN 3-89821-574-1

4   *Paul Fox and Koray Melikoğlu (eds.)*
    Formal Investigations
    Aesthetic Style in Late-Victorian and Edwardian Detective Fiction
    ISBN 978-3-89821-593-0

5   *David Ellis*
    Writing Home
    Black Writing in Britain Since the War
    ISBN 978-3-89821-591-6

6   *Wei H. Kao*
    The Formation of an Irish Literary Canon in the Mid-Twentieth Century
    ISBN 978-3-89821-545-9

7   *Bianca Del Villano*
    Ghostly Alterities
    Spectrality and Contemporary Literatures in English
    ISBN 978-3-89821-714-9

8   *Melanie Ann Hanson*
    Decapitation and Disgorgement
    The Female Body's Text in Early Modern English Drama and Poetry
    ISBN 978-3-89821-605-5

9   *Shafquat Towheed (ed.)*
    New Readings in the Literature of British India, c.1780-1947
    ISBN 978-3-89821-673-9

10 *Paola Baseotto*
    "Disdeining life, desiring leaue to die"
    Spenser and the Psychology of Despair
    ISBN 978-3-89821-567-1

11 *Annie Gagiano*
    Dealing with Evils
    Essays on Writing from Africa
    ISBN 978-3-89821-867-2

Thomas F. Halloran

JAMES JOYCE DEVELOPING IRISH IDENTITY

A Study of the Development
of Postcolonial Irish Identity in the Novels
of James Joyce

ibidem-Verlag
Stuttgart

Bibliografische Information der Deutschen Nationalbibliothek
Die Deutsche Nationalbibliothek verzeichnet diese Publikation in der Deutschen Nationalbibliografie; detaillierte bibliografische Daten sind im Internet über http://dnb.d-nb.de abrufbar.

Bibliographic information published by the Deutsche Nationalbibliothek
Die Deutsche Nationalbibliothek lists this publication in the Deutsche Nationalbibliografie; detailed bibliographic data are available in the Internet at http://dnb.d-nb.de.

Cover illustration: Alisa Blanter

∞

Gedruckt auf alterungsbeständigem, säurefreien Papier
Printed on acid-free paper

ISSN: 1614-4651

ISBN-10: 3-89821-571-7
ISBN-13: 978-3-89821-571-8

© *ibidem*-Verlag
Stuttgart 2009

Alle Rechte vorbehalten

Das Werk einschließlich aller seiner Teile ist urheberrechtlich geschützt. Jede Verwertung außerhalb der engen Grenzen des Urheberrechtsgesetzes ist ohne Zustimmung des Verlages unzulässig und strafbar. Dies gilt insbesondere für Vervielfältigungen, Übersetzungen, Mikroverfilmungen und elektronische Speicherformen sowie die Einspeicherung und Verarbeitung in elektronischen Systemen.

All rights reserved. No part of this publication may be reproduced, stored in or introduced into a retrieval system, or transmitted, in any form, or by any means (electronic, mechanical, photocopying, recording or otherwise) without the prior written permission of the publisher. Any person who does any unauthorized act in relation to this publication may be liable to criminal prosecution and civil claims for damages.

Printed in Germany

CONTENTS

Acknowledgements

Preface

Introduction   1

Chapter 1
Postcolonial Status   9

Chapter 2
The Articulation of Colonial Irish Identity in *Dubliners*: Homogeneity as Productive of Fantasy and Materialism instead of Idealism   33

Chapter 3
The Evolution of Stephen Dedalus and Irish Identity: The Allegory of Personal and National Liberation in *A Portrait of the Artist as a Young Man* and *Stephen Hero*   67

Chapter 4
An Alternative Definition of Irish Identity: Stephen, History and Bloom's Inclusive Irishness   103

Conclusion   143

Bibliography   149

Acknowledgements

I have heard fellow academics refer to their research projects as "my baby." Indeed, at times this study has demanded the time, effort and patience that a child might demand of its parents. Continuing this analogy, as I have assumed the role of father/mother for this study (now there's a Joycean concept for you), I must first pay my respects, to the man who could only be described as "the Godfather," Dr. Eugene O'Brien. Eugene has done everything that could be asked of a supervisor and a friend. I am truly grateful to Eugene for setting me onto this path of research and learning that I know I am so lucky to have.

Of course this project is indebted to its extended family as well, namely all of my friends and relatives in Ireland, France, and the USA. I would also like to express my personal gratitude to Mary Immaculate College. Extra thanks are due to: Grainne, Angus and Eoin who were great colleagues at Mary I. I must also thank the English Department as a whole, Florrie, Gerry, John Mac and John Scaggs, for each was providing valuable mentoring in everything from teaching, to correcting, to study and research. I would like to also thank the James Joyce Summer School for granting me the opportunity to listen to and speak with so many like-minded individuals. I am also grateful for the cover art provided by Alisa Blanter.

I would like to thank the editors of *New Voices in Irish Studies* 5 and *In-between: Essays & Studies in Literary Criticism* for publishing earlier versions of ideas also expressed in this book. Finally, I would like to thank Ibidem-Verlag, particularly Valerie Lange, for giving me this opportunity to share my work.

Preface

> We cannot help making the attempt to come to the end of a reading, to reach a stable point where it all makes coherent sense, and we should never stop trying to achieve this moment; but it is an endlessly repeated failure to do so. (Attridge, *Cambridge Companion* 3)

Derek Attridge is writing about the impossibility of providing the definitive interpretation of *Finnegans Wake*, but it could just as easily apply to any project that seeks to summarise or define the Joycean *oeuvre*. The goal of this study is to re-imagine Joyce's work and thus provide a new way of understanding the way that we think about postcolonial criticism and Irish identity.

This thesis finds postcolonial criticism as a theoretical approach capable of offering insightful analysis for the study of Irish identity and a useful new analysis of Joyce. This study makes it apparent that postcolonial theory must recognise Ireland if it is to continue usefully to interpret the literature and cultures of other postcolonial nations.

Through close reading of *Dubliners*, *A Portrait of the Artist as a Young Man*, *Stephen Hero* and *Ulysses*, Joyce develops an articulation of the problems that colonialism poses to the nation-state without the right to create identity autonomously. This study provides a reading of these texts and develops the postcolonial concepts that arise in Joyce's *oeuvre* years before other postcolonial writers would attempt similar tasks for their nations and cultures. This study will provide the reader with a new perspective on Joyce's international influence through postcolonial literature.

Introduction
Stories of a Developing Identity

> The first Normans landed in Wexford in May 1169. That was the beginning of the political struggle between England and Ireland which was to dominate Irish history until the present day. (Ó hEithir 25)

A strand of modern Irish history mythologises the 800 years prior to Irish independence from the British Empire as a period of struggle and war for autonomy, until finally, sovereignty for the Free State was accomplished in 1922. However, as Declan Kiberd argues, the creation of an independent Ireland caused problems for one of the first decolonising nations. Most importantly for this thesis, these issues involved the necessity of changing national thinking from a war-like mentality of "us" versus "them," to a more open and forward-thinking notion of "us," defined in terms of relation to the outside world. It appears that after such an extended period of Ireland's nationalistic exertions, the general consciousness in Ireland had come to firmly identify with the ideals of the nationalist movement that espoused the self-created construction of a homogenising power, and such a creation would prove difficult to deconstruct.

The nationalist movement was successful because of its ability to unite the different nation-wide political and social agendas and then produce a convergence for the cause of independence. Nationalism had forged a bond throughout Ireland by way of a self-created version of the Irish national history that effectively homogenised its citizens with the intention of creating a unified voice for a societal decolonisation of English imperialism. When the nation was created, the need for this homogenisation was over, and the deconstruction of such a powerful aspect of national consciousness was necessary if a more pluralist form of national growth were to be encouraged. As difficult as this task might seem, it would be important in terms of altering the national way of thinking. The early Free State governments of Eamon de Valera and Sean Lemass did not re-think the nationalist outlook but attempted to protect national interest and sovereignty by further isolating Ireland. However, banning English products, censoring foreign literature and later censoring any national literature that did not fit the restrictive ideals upon which a new Ireland was to be founded, created a nation that could not cope with change.

Ireland's post-independence founders created a national ideal based on a backwards look at a certain version of Irish history and its people, and found an extension of this created vision of "Irishness" more enticing than the prospects of a present Irish community that was ravaged by war and split by the differences that complicated Irish culture in terms of its core values. These areas included the question of the national language, as well as that of the nation's role in the international community, and specifically with respect to England. A further issue was the extent to which the Catholic Church dictated the morality of governmental policy. There was also the question as to what role the minority could play in the existing restrictive national definition. Rather than answer these difficult questions in the government of the new nation, Ireland stalled the problem by defining the Irish as the inverse of the English. Kiberd explains:

> The newly liberated people would be employing the unmodified devices of the old regime upon themselves. War and civil war appeared to have drained all energy and imagination away: there was precious little left with

which to reimagine the national condition. (Kiberd, *Inventing* 263)

The above illustrates the need for an independent creation of "Irishness" by the Irish in what came to be their postcolonial situation, rather than making the mistake of simplifying Irish identity in terms of its being defined as non-English.

The Irish Free State and early Republic were founded on the misguided idea of a closed community that had never existed anywhere but in lines of poetry or perhaps worse, of political propaganda.[1] Ireland was never an exclusive nation of one language, one religion, one ethnicity and one culture, but was mythologically imagined to have such a history in a time of pre-colonial freedom. The combination of attributes including Gaelic ancestry, the Roman Catholic religion, and a rural "west of Ireland" ideology of identity, created confusion and alienation for the vast majority which could not fit into all of these moulds.

Although the early Irish government created a binary anti-English definition for the Irish, Ireland's writers would debate the problem of a successful revolution that lacked a proper ideology to reinforce it. Ironically, those writers who first voiced this need for an ever-changing hybrid definition of Irishness were largely disregarded and condemned as "anti-Irish" by the new state apparatus of the Free State. In order to change the unrealistic self-perception of the nation, writers of the Free State, most significantly James Joyce, re-envisioned the nation in other terms than those sponsored by the dominating powers of imperialism, church and state. Joyce's foresight of the problems of an ongoing Irish

---

[1] For this perspective one only needs to consult D. P. Moran, discussed in Willard Potts, *Joyce and the Two Irelands*, or Douglas Hyde's speech "The Necessity for De-Anglicizing Ireland."

nationalism in the Free State develops throughout the entirety of his work. From *Dubliners*, where he scrutinises the problems of the colonial situation, to his conclusive *Finnegans Wake*, where the author attempts to deconstruct the problems of postcoloniality, Joyce is ever concerned with the identity issues that arise as a direct result of British and Roman imperialism and its ensuing follower, Irish nationalism.

Before dealing directly with Joyce's constructions and deconstructions of imperialism, it is necessary to answer questions about the very nature of the postcolonial approach to literature in the first place. First of, what is postcolonialism/postcolonial literature and theory? In Dane Kennedy's words, postcolonial studies have

> [r]aised provocative, often fundamental, questions about the epistemological structures of power between metropolitan and colonial societies, about the construction of group identities in the context of state formation, even about the nature and uses of historical evidence itself.
>
> (356)

This study takes postcolonialism on for the benefits described above. Furthermore, Ireland has proved particularly controversial because of its existence in both "first-world" and "third world" canons.[2] Therefore, it seems increasingly necessary that Joyce, who stands in the crossroads of seemingly all theories, categorisations, groupings, listings and canons, should be studied from an

---

[2] Graham and Maley note that Ireland, "so susceptible to binaries, undoes the double bind of West and rest"(Graham and Maley 151). They continue that Ireland should remind postcolonial studies that the binary of "West" and "rest" must be regarded carefully, as Ireland exists in both spaces.

angle that seeks to investigate these boundaries and liminal spaces. Taking a cue from Colin Graham and Willy Maley's editing of the *Irish Studies Review* issue on postcolonial theory, this study's objectives are quite similar with an interest in raising the following issues:

> the 'uniqueness' of Irish postcolonialism; the 'binary' as a dominant mode of thinking in Irish contexts, the possible differences in an Irish setting, between 'literary' or 'cultural' models of postcolonial criticism, and the various ways in which themes of postcolonial – ambivalence, authenticity, diaspora, difference, hybridity, migrancy, mimicry, nativism, signifying and subalternity – can work to counteract the exclusive and negative aspects of identity politics. (149)

Of course the major difference is that this project looks exclusively at how some of these concepts of postcolonial theory apply to Joyce's body of work and only touches on the implications for Irish Studies and postcolonial literature.

This relatively new method of literary theory has gained wide acceptance for the literature of the decolonised nations of Africa and the sub-continent of India, the Caribbean and to a lesser extent South America. However, the few examples of European postcolonials, namely Ireland, Greece, Catalonia and the Basque Country are rarely, if ever included in studies of postcolonialism. Trouble arises for the postcolonial categorisation of the newly independent Irish nation, mainly because Ireland has been internationally perceived as having so many similarities to its former coloniser, England. Because of the colour of the Irish people's skin, the dominance of the English language and movement between the countries, not to mention their close proximity and because the Irish participated in the imperial endeavour, Ireland has often been linked with the coloniser, more often than regarded as a colony itself.

Recent scholarship in Irish studies has made important strides to help give recognition to Ireland's role as an early model in the discourses of decolonisation and postcolonialism. In these studies, the problems of classifying the Irish experience as postcolonial also arise, but because of the unique aspects of the situation and circumstances, and most importantly the contribution on the part of Irish literature, this study argues for the vital need to incorporate the Irish and most specifically Joyce into the field of postcolonial literature.

The first section of this study traces the major issues that arise in the acceptance and importance of Irish postcoloniality. Because the Irish role in postcolonialism is that of pioneer and outsider in comparison with the former faraway colonies, Ireland does not fit with more recognisable decolonised nations and attention is also given to the problems with Irish postcoloniality and postcolonial theory that have become complicated because of this unique situation. This first chapter seeks to provide an explanation of postcolonial studies as related to Ireland, to examine the benefits and difficulties, but ultimately the necessity of this synergy.

The next aspect of the study moves from an expressly theoretical angle to a combination of theory and close reading in a study of Joyce's unique reaction to colonialism. While this thesis may add to the increasingly developing area of "Joyce studies" overall, a gap remains in Joyce studies in terms of postcolonialism, in that recent scholarship has yet to include the modern identity questions of contemporary Ireland in relation to Joyce's *oeuvre*. In *Joyce, Race and Empire*, Vincent J. Cheng has noticed that until recently Joyce has not been regarded as anything but a writer concerned with style above all, as well as being deemed to be devoid of a political message. Expanding on this aspect of Joyce studies, this thesis will be joining Joyce's critical ideas about British colonialism with those of the mainstream contemporary postcolonial criticism. To do this, the second chapter examines *Dubliners*, reading the collection as presenting a nation lost in inarticulate fantasy or conversely the mimicry of materialism which frames the problems of a colonised nation afraid to create itself independently. The third chapter studies the articulation of the desire to control one's own identity as expressed by Stephen Dedalus in *Portrait of an Artist as a Young Man* and *Stephen Hero*. The final chapter provides a study of *Ulysses* that highlights the colonial trappings of Irish identity and the possibility of freedom that exists and is eventually articulated and realised by Leopold Bloom.

This study finds Joyce to have taken an extraordinarily progressive stance on decolonisation, by comprehending the need for nationalism and yet also acknowledging the necessity for the deconstruction of this vehicle for independence. Joyce's innovations in style have a postcolonial aim as well, more complicated than just a post-modern writing technique, namely the deconstruction of the English language, and the promotion of the hybrid language that develops in *Ulysses* and especially in *Finnegans Wake*, which is a template for the former colonies to use English and the novel tradition in an independent way.

Moving beyond Joyce's deconstruction of the English language and tradition, the question for contemporary Irish studies becomes: "What is Irishness?" Joyce's deconstruction of the traditions leads to benefits for society in terms of hybridity, fluidity, and openness. But what consequences have these changes had for modern Irish identity? What makes up the national definition after postcolonialism is a question just beginning to be asked let alone answered and it is fitting that one of the first countries to decolonise would be among the first to find itself at a crossroads of identity in its evolution. This book seeks to encourage the study of Ireland for the scholar interested in postcolonialism and world literature.

Chapter 1
Postcolonial Status

History is written by the victor

> *History* is what gets written down in books by life's winners and *tradition* is what gets remembered and told among the common people. (Kiberd, *Inventing* 15)

> That branch of knowledge which deals with past events, as recorded in writings or otherwise ascertained. (*Oxford English Dictionary*)

The postcolonial theoretical approach to literature may involve more connections with history than most literary and cultural theoretical methodologies (Lloyd, *Ireland* 5-19). History, in a traditional Western academic sense, is reduced to linear time-line testimony, aimed at providing an unambiguous narrative, a reductive representation of the past through the historians' reconstruction. However, history in postcolonial theory is too large to be all-inclusive and too random to conform to a scientifically recorded set of events, constructed upon the idea of progress. In fact, the very idea of a universal truism such as "progress" is suspect within the postcolonial paradigm. Luke Gibbons has defined that what the historian should now fear is, "history itself, particularly when it is not easily incorporated into the controlling, seamless narratives that allow communities to smooth over, or even to deny, their own pasts" (17). Western philosophy assumes that the nation state is the successful fulfilment of a universal aspiration, the national developmental process of nationhood. By this method there is only one strand of history that is analysed, that being the path to nation-statehood (Lloyd, *Inventing* 24). Furthermore, history analyses the perspective of the victor or as Seamus Heaney stated: "It is difficult at times to repress the thought that history is about as instructive as an abattoir; that Tacitus was right and that peace is merely the desolation left behind after the decisive operations of merciless power" (456).

However, postcolonial critics have questioned this universalism on the grounds that this notion of history not only is a Western presentation but more importantly a Eurocentric force that influences the other's perspective into accepting the Western notion of history.[3] This destabilising imperative has prompted critics of postcolonial theory to question the relevance of any theory that cannot answer such finite problems as: "when is a postcolonial period ever set to begin or end?" (McClintock 85). As a theoretically driven discourse, postcolonial theory is constantly critiquing its own givens and assumptions. However, this very question illustrates the possibility of an alternative non-linear narrative that could be realised to incorporate the multifaceted representations of the past.

History is a principal tool of academic learning and a fundamental source of knowledge, but historical study must be interrogated in terms of its assumptions if it is to do justice to the complexity of perspectives that require to be taken into account. The ideal tactic proffered for creating authority and legitimising power is history; by few other means can claims be made in Western thinking than through the power of verified historical fact. History therefore becomes the breeding ground of nationalism through "monoculturalism, ancestry, purity of race and lineage" (Ashcroft, *Em-*

---

[3] Because of this scepticism of history, postcolonial theory is susceptible to wrath of the historical studies that sees postcolonialism as primarily attacking their field. Yet hopefully readers will not misconstrue the point that postcolonial theory aims to expand the study of history to include other voices, without an intent to silence any.

pire 154). These ideological constructs of the old European world served as justification for the colonial project and the domination of the other. The nation with colonial aspirations needs to legitimise its claims through history, and this promotes the interpretative histories that only seek to benefit one nation's cause (Said, *Culture* 16). To return to the opening quote from Kiberd, however, there is another area through which identity can be enunciated, and that is the realm of literature and tradition. Identity and tradition are the areas of culture, and culture "is the site on which the struggle for hegemony takes place, the discourses are the primary cultural means through which individuals become subjects" (Cairns and Richards 15). To this point Gibbons adds that "identity does not just involve consciousness, or even self-consciousness, but also the realm of representation, i.e., the capacity to be realised in material form" (Gibbons, *Transformations* 10). Meaning that the articulation of national identity is a nationwide struggle that must be discussed in national literature, as a national culture is essential to nationality and nationhood. The issue arises then as to whether there is any superior approach to the question of nationality and identity for the former colonies than through the institution of literature? Edward Said notes:

> The main battle in imperialism is over land, of course; but when it came to who owned the land, who had the right to settle and work on it, who kept it going, who won it back, and who now plans its future – these issues were reflected, contested and even for a time decided in narrative. (*Culture* xiii)

Said promotes literature as one of the prime methods for the postcolonial nation to achieve autonomy of identity: to write in response to the coloniser or to ignore the coloniser and return to the pre-colonial are the only options. However, to ignore history and specifically the history of colonisation not only denies reality, it also denies modernisation in a vain and stubborn refusal of the altering consciousness of the national populace. The postcolonial nation has little to gain by ignoring the past and much to lose by ignoring what is a shared national experience of colonisation. However, equally dangerous perhaps is the embrace of the decolonising nationalism that polarises the national identity. Lloyd explains:

> For if the state relies, in the postcolonial moment, on the canonisation of a certain selection of practices then termed traditions and forges that canon through nationalist histories, it relies equally on a violence proportional in intensity and kind to the resistance it meets in order to repress or erase the traces of other practices and narratives.
>
> (*Ireland* 82)

The postcolonial writer realises the situation and offers a voice to the people who have been represented by the coloniser prior to the opportunity to "hear" their own perspective but there is also a responsibility to include a response that can be creative of a more flexible paradigm of the nation's identity now that an initially anti-colonialist identity has been achieved. It is by allowing the national consciousness to have some freedom of identity, Lloyd argues, that national projects such as a conscious modernisation of the culture/nation can begin.

The problem with offering a voice to the newly liberated is that the voice is also speaking to Europe and as a result is forced to speak in the coloniser's language. The damage that the coloniser's language has left on a national pride, psychology and development is a seminal factor in the psyche of all former colonies, and the postcolonial writer in this language often suffers through this situation, neither a part of the colonising process, nor a traditional version of the national artist. For this reason the postcolonial writer in English is often the first to take up the role as a hybrid.

England's English

Prior to postcolonial studies, writing in English from the colonies of the former Empire was located at the periphery of English literature and culture or Commonwealth Literature of the 1960s and 1970s. Literature in English from abroad was meant to fit into the canon if it emulated the technical qualities of its English contemporaries and could be valued by the standards of traditional literary criticism. While these categorisations not only undermine the artistic integrity of postcolonial writing, they also ignore the multicultural possibilities that could be incorporated into the tradition of prose fiction. More subversively, the creation of a hierarchy that promotes England's literature as superior to that of the colonies creates a counter-revolutionary mindset in the colonised. Gibbons makes this point in stating that for the colonised

> [t]o win recognition and gain respectability, emergent nationalisms in subaltern cultures have tended to mimic their master's voices and reproduce in their own idioms the closed, univocal expressions of identity articulated in the imperial centre. (*Transformations* 7)

The idea is that even in a nationalist movement the mindset is still colonised, therefore for the colonial/postcolonial writer the task becomes increasingly difficult in that they will often have to write beyond the limitations of colonialism as well as the restrictions of a nationalism that is likewise interested in narrowing the discourse of national identity.

Postcolonial writers deal with the obstacle of using the English language because the "main feature of imperial oppression is control of language" (Ashcroft, *Empire* 7). The control of language leads to the standard version of metropolitan England's English being installed in the educational system of the colonial nation; this development ensconces standard English in the postcolonial nation as the ideal instrument of communication and self-definition. Furthermore, this develops a hierarchy of class that is arranged in relation to the idealised centre, which of course is England.

This problematic of English language develops substantially when applied to literature, as the standard version of English, as a normative value, begins to affect the position in which national literatures are evaluated, so that the coloniser speaks with such authority "that no aspect of the identity of the colonised can safely be assumed to be inherent" (Cairns and Richards 8). This control serves to intimidate the colonised into subservience to England's language. What is more, Ashcroft details the problem with standardising one form of British English as the Literature of England imposes the norms for all literatures in English. Here Ashcroft describes how the canon shapes our perception of "good" language:

> through the literary canon, the body of British texts which all too frequently still acts as a touchstone of taste and value, and through RS-English (Received Standard English), which asserts the English of south-east England as a universal norm, the weight of antiquity continues to dominate cultural production in much of the post-colonial world. (Ashcroft et al., *Empire* 7)

1 Postcolonial Status   15

The postcolonial writer must first advocate a reworking of literature in English to provide a voice for his/her nation. However, to first make the English language their own, the writer must create a literature that would be independently specific to their nation, and not merely an offshoot of, or subject to, the English tradition and standards. Yet for the postcolonial writer's work to be considered it must to original, while still being a part of the English language. David Cairns and Shaun Richards illustrate in their interpretation of Shakespeare's history play *Henry V* the necessity of Irish accent that is marked, but still comprehensible to the English ear:

> The Welsh, Scots and Irish, must, therefore, be seen to speak English as evidence of their incorporation within the greater might of England, but they must speak it with enough deviations from the standard form to make their subordinate status in the union manifestly obvious. What cannot be acknowledged is their possession of an alternative language and culture, for to do so would be to stage the presence of the very contradictions which the play denies in its attempt to stage the ideal of a unified English Nation State. (11)

This passage demonstrates the revolutionary change that postcolonial theory attempts to promote. Whereas the hybridity of language in Shakespeare could be interpreted as a positive control apparatus to keep the colonised in subservience, postcolonial discourse will seek to create linguistic hybridity, especially through postcolonial readings that employ a poststructuralist methodology, i.e. Homi Bhabha and Gayatri Chakravorty Spivak. Essentially:

> There are now many people in all parts of the world who see English as having become detached from Britain or

Britishness. They claim the language as their own property, for they have moulded and refashioned it to make it bear the weight of their own experience. (Drabble 809)

But before language can be detached from Britain, postcolonial studies needs to decide what constitutes the notion of "Great Britain" as a nation as well as probing the constitutive conditions of the canon of "English" Literature.

Re-visioning "English" literature

The postcolonial writer must realise the importance of the written word and the tradition of literature if a meaningful response to the coloniser is to be made. However, in this response the writer is already at a disadvantage as the language and tradition of Great Britain are implied. Frantz Fanon comments that when the postcolonial writer "is anxiously trying to create a cultural work he fails to realise that he is utilising techniques and language which are borrowed from the stranger in his country" (Fanon 180). This situation creates difficulty for postcolonial writers who want to respond to the colonised representation of their nation and culture and yet also must demonstrate their mastery of the colonial tradition. All of which puts the postcolonial writers in the complicated position of having to accurately translate their culture into the language and tradition of the coloniser. However, forging the confidence to make the English language and literature the national culture of the postcolonial nation is a site of struggle as "[i]t is only when hybridity becomes truly reciprocal rather than hierarchical that the encounter with the culture of the coloniser ceases to be detrimental to one's development" (Gibbons, *Transformations* 180).

1 Postcolonial Status   17

The postcolonial writer is gambling that the coloniser will acknowledge their writing, because to go unrecognised by their own nation for writing in a foreign language and tradition is already difficult. In taking on such a project, the postcolonial writer is investing a tremendous power in language and in its ability to convey a culture. On this issue, Attridge remarks that one of the values of Joyce is in reading how he embraces the persuasive influence of language:

> The blandishments of a wooing sailor with stories of a better life on the other side of the globe are a very long way from chauvinist and militarist propaganda, but what can be learned, so pleasurably, from Joyce's critical explorations of the potency of fiction and rhetoric within specific social and economic contexts may help to sharpen the linguistic and conceptual vigilance needed to combat the totalising and totalitarian manipulations of language and thought still powerful today. (*Cambridge Companion* 9-10)

The postcolonial writer must understand the power and history of language in order to use language and literature to explore ideas about nationality and identity. Joyce, as Attridge articulates, sees the opportunity to demonstrate language's powerful ability and then twist this power to make language speak for the colonised.

Postcolonial studies are designed to re-vision the non-Western world of "otherness" and exoticism. In accounting for the literature of England and its presentation of Ireland, Cairns and Richard note:

> Writing by Englishmen about Ireland and the Irish may not have served to broaden English knowledge of the

neighbouring island and its inhabitants, but also to define the qualities of 'Englishness' by simultaneously defining 'not-English' or otherness. (2)

Representations of Ireland by the coloniser are intentionally and unintentionally biased, but ultimately leaving the colonised spoken for and hence speechless. Postcolonial literature retells history from the alternative or suppressed perspective, giving readers the opportunity to find a balance between the multiple perspectives. Through this method, not only is history reclaimed by the postcolonial nation, but also national consciousnesses are envisioned and the institution of English literature is expanded into a medium of transformative communication rather viewed as merely one nation's literature.

Furthermore, Denis Walder explains, that the aim, "of postcolonial theory, whatever its origins, is to aid, not hinder critical understanding of a proliferating area of literary creativity, as well as the reinterpretation of text from a newly aware position" (79). Postcolonial theory, like postcolonial literature, is founded on the goal of freeing literature in English from a restrictive notion of the English tradition, thus making the language something of a shared medium between nations while never belonging exclusively to any one nation specifically. Walder also mentions the questions of reinterpretation. With the inclusion of postcolonial novels and theoretical texts to the traditional canon, the traditionally canonised novel must be re-evaluated in respect to the postcolonial novel.

Creative growth by the postcolonial national writer not only takes the form of re-vision, but also in a vision itself, the ability to see the future of the nation in terms previously unimagined. What writers like W. B. Yeats or Joyce can do is to ignore the colonial occupation, the actual colonial setting, and create visions of a new setting:

> Art in this context might be seen as man's constant effort to create for himself a different order of reality from that which is given to him: against the ability to imagine things as they are, it counterpoises the capacity to imagine things as they might be. (Kiberd, *Inventing* 118)

Kiberd focuses on the question of re-imagining Ireland from a postcolonial theoretical perspective, in a manner similar to Joyce, who imagines an Ireland unconnected to an exclusive vision of the past, when Stephen Dedalus attempts to fly by the nets of nationality, language, and religion (Joyce, *Portrait* 220).

"An Éirinneach nó Sassanach tú?"

Here ensues the apparent difficulty of the Irish situation in terms of the canon of English literature. *The Oxford Companion to English Literature* offers this invitation to the postcolonial study of Irish literature: "Post-colonial literature consists of a body of writing emanating from Europe's former colonies which addresses questions of history, identity, ethnicity, gender and language" (Drabble 808). Indeed, this study makes the argument that this definition could be rewritten, "Joycean literature consists of a body of writing emanating from Great Britain's former colony Ireland, which addresses questions of history, identity, ethnicity, gender and language." Admittedly the themes of the Joycean *oeuvre* do not warrant postcolonial inclusion in themselves, but excluding Joyce from this dialogue based on Ireland's geographic position and race is likewise inadvisable. Unlike African and Asian colonial writers who were at the periphery of the English canon of literature, the colonial United Kingdom claimed Irish-born and Irish-themed writers as their own. Even fellow Caucasians and English descendants like the American, Canadian, Australian and New Zealand born or based writers were viewed as being specific to their location and nation or colonial state. However, the Irish writers, although subjects of the U.K., no different in name than other colonial subjects further afield, were consistently anthologised as English writers. James Joyce famously derided what might have been intended as a compliment from the English perspective, his inclusion into their canon:

> And in spite of everything Ireland remains the brain of the United Kingdom. The English, judiciously practical and ponderous, furnish the over-stuffed stomach of humanity with a perfect gadget – the water closet. The Irish, condemned to express themselves in a language not their own, have stamped on it the mark of their own genius and compete for glory with the civilised nations. This is then called English literature. (Ellmann 226)

Joyce's sarcastic comments highlight Ireland's unwillingness to be made English, or to be exploited like other colonial nations. Adding to Joyce's frustration is the inclusion of Ireland's identity within the context of Great Britain.

By inserting the language question into this statement, Joyce not only links the Irish experience with that of other colonials, but further insults the English canon of which he does not wish to be a part. The language question is exploited here to draw attention to the differences between national identities. Yet despite the refusal to be English by law, definition, style or subject, contemporary scholarship continues to link the separate and independent nations of Ireland and Great Britain.

Irish postcoloniality

The Empire Writes Back (Ashcroft et al.) was the seminal students' guide to postcolonial theory; however, the study insensitively portrayed the Irish nation's understanding of its own history as involving a somewhat lacklustre membership of the United Kingdom. From the opening chapter of the study's discussion of models of postcolonialism, it is suggested that Ireland's "subsequent complicity in the British imperial enterprise makes it difficult for colonised peoples outside Britain to accept their [Irish] identity as post-colonial" (33). There is no doubt that the Irish colonial experience was different to their African and Asian counterparts, or that the Irish at times benefited as a result of their closer colonial ties with England than those of other colonial states. But to overlook the Irish resentment at, and challenge to, colonisation is to disregard a significant aspect of Irish history and national development. The absence of any reference to Irish writers outside of Yeats (who is essentially viewed as an English writer by the study), the problem of Ireland's position with respect to postcolonial legitimacy begins.

Perhaps because of the length of the English stay in Ireland, the geographic and racial proximity, and some similarities in culture (despite constant polarisation based on binary oppositional definition of each other), the Irish are often regarded as English in the international community. In spite of this, the identity debate that exists within the culture of the two islands has often dominated their relationship. Irish identity, particularly before and just after independence, was largely based on what was not English or what was Gaelic. This line of thinking not only seems to comply with Fanon's ideas of postcolonial development, but also strengthens the legitimacy of Irish postcolonial claims. Essentially Ireland has developed in parallel with England, but has also developed differently, so that the two nations cannot be joined by the colonial history to the extent that an Irish writer could represent England.

It is useful again to consider Lloyd's criticism, which continues some of the previously detailed postcolonial interests in the way of historical study. Lloyd posits the idea of the unilateral limitations of history and applies it to Irish history, which proves particularly successful because:

> That [. . .] agrarian movements, women's movements, labour movements, to name only a few[,] have largely been occluded by the dominant forms and debates of Irish history is an effect of the organizing concerns of official history: the formation of the nation and state; the narrative of political institutions and state apparatuses; in short, the modernization of Ireland. (*Ireland* 37)

Lloyd's point is that the development of modern Ireland by way of independence and state departments has overlooked the role of the many movements that contributed to the creation of contemporary Ireland. The encapsulation of Irish history links unrelated movements and occludes movements that seem to have played a role in the shaping of the nation and only by questioning "official" histories can the full story of Irish history begin. Gibbons continues this idea of history's occlusion of the "full story" by adding, "the justified criticism of nationalism as masking over internal divisions, inventing tradition, or retreating into xenophobia and racialism, is properly directed at the classical European model [more so than Ireland]" (Gibbons, *Transformations* 153). Gibbons' point is that the distortions of Irish history are not necessarily a result of nationalism's desire to consciously corrupt our understanding of the past, but a result of colonisation and the unbalanced modernisation of a colony trying, problematically, to be both a postcolonial nation and an ever-independent great nation of the past in the same league as their coloniser.

Finally, Ireland fits into the postcolonial concept if for no other reason than because its writers say so. Consider Heaney's comment:

> The child in the bedroom listening simultaneously to the domestic idiom of his Irish home and the official idioms of the British broadcaster while picking up from behind both signals of some other distress, that child was already being schooled for the complexities of his adult predicament, a future where he would have to adjudicate among promptings variously ethical, aesthetical, moral, political, metrical, sceptical, cultural, topical, typical, post-colonial and taken altogether, simply impossible. (452)

The Irish national consciousness has long seen itself as oppressed by its English coloniser and despite differences between the types of oppression in other colonies, Irish history will continue to include its own story of British oppression. Ireland's politics, from the Act of Union, through De Valera's economic war, has centred around the Irish-English relationship that had until 1922 been voiced in Westminster. Even Irish independence has failed to distance the nation's identity questions. The nationalist movement that led to independence, that created the free state, also confined the nation's political interests to those that shared a confining nationalist and religious position, effectively based on an inverse of English rule yet strangely mimicking it. Furthermore, Ireland since the arrival of the English has seen unprecedented transformations in culture. Perhaps only the Caribbean colonies have seen greater changes and more forced hybridity than Ireland. Although not all of these changes in Irish culture can be attributed to colonialism, the changes began with English influence.

Denying Irish postcoloniality

Gibbons has speculated that the problem with Ireland and postcolonial studies is simply that "a native population which happened to be white was an affront to the very idea of 'white man's burden', and threw into disarray some of the constitutive categories of colonial discourse" (*Transformations* 149). Perhaps it is simply this problem that prevents Irish inclusion in what would otherwise constitute a coherent paradigm for a common understanding of "postcolonial." The objections to Irish postcolonialism also arrive from a political angle as the ignorance of Ireland in *The Empire Writes Back* is also mirrored in the polemical writing of Liam Kennedy.[4] Kennedy's position attempts to deny Irish aspirations to postcolonial inclusion by inverting the assertion into an argument that actually incorporates Ireland within English centrality. Kennedy poses that "Ireland, in effect, was a junior partner in that vast exploitative enterprise known as the British Empire" (176). While inconclusive "evidence" is provided with regards to Irish roles in the empire, Kennedy conveniently ignores the role that the subaltern, and other generally accepted postcolonial

---

[4] It may be true of all academic disciplines, but Graham and Maley note that "there is a resistance to theory on the part of some 'nationalist', 'liberal' and 'revisionist' critics when theory is perceived as challenging their own views in which the postcolonial has been caught up in these pre-existing debates which has both promoted and stifled postcolonial theory's Irish existence so far" (150). Liam Kennedy merely represents one voice from the revisionist or unionist angle, and it should be acknowledged that equally biased interpretations of postcolonialism exist from other politically charged positions as noted in the above quotation.

states, played in supporting the British Empire's mission. Furthermore, by only representing the history of the Unionist perspective, Kennedy neglects the objections that have generally been made on behalf of Irish support of such issues as Home Rule, non-conscription to the World Wars, the land acts, the language question and the Gaelic sport movement.

Kennedy defines Irish colonial history as specific to the mid-seventeenth century, and attempts to prove by way of graphs and diagrams that Ireland is not a postcolonial nation (167-173). In a plethora of contrivances, Kennedy seems to link Ireland with statistics to other Western European nations rather than to traditional postcolonial African and Asian nations. However, it has been noted by Lloyd that Kennedy ignores the individual representations of Irish life and consciousness and even from a factual point of view: "Ireland's underdevelopment in relation to other small European nations" which was well known, is not adduced, as this fact "was attributed usually to British rule" (Lloyd, *Ireland* 9). Lloyd also notes Kennedy's failure to account for Irish emigration, the negative effects this had on the Irish labour pool, the landscape of the country, the psychological damage to the nation,[5] more importantly, Kennedy's would have been more similar to

---

[5] While this essay finds Lloyd's criticism useful, and wholly admits the "emotional" dimension to postcolonial studies, it is an area often attacked by critics wary of what appears to them as a hidden Irish nationalism. For example Bruce Stewart's review of Kiberd fumes, "the kind of cultural nationalism that fills the pages of *Inventing Ireland*, and the even simpler kind on which it draws for emotional and intellectual sustenance, seems to me to obscure, narrow, and misrepresent the actual experience of reading modern Irish writing" (5). Although this project has tried not to adopt a political stance, it seems it will be read with one.

African and Asian statistics had the Irish not been in a position to emigrate (*Ireland* 10-12).

However flawed Kennedy's study may be, a fair warning is made in regards to the justification of postcolonial research: "In terms of the colonial/postcolonial debate, one needs to show precisely how this model illuminates our understanding of past and present, and the relative importance of any insights gained" (178). Kennedy's comment is intended to discourage the intersection of postcolonial studies and the Irish case, but while this objection is impractical, it will serve to help define and clarify the aim of this research. To reject Ireland's postcolonial status is to undermine the postcolonial literary project of other national literatures. Ireland's postcolonial status can make no claims to being the same as another colonial situation, but no colonial situation is exactly the same. What is more important than establishing guidelines as to what the cut off points are for official recognition of postcoloniality, is the recognition of how Irish writing, like Irish independence, has centred around identity. Also worth considering is a point ironically made by historians James Livesay and Stuart Murray, that postcolonial studies may have a tendency to create a narrative about colonial Ireland that ignores the complexities of history. These critics state of *Inventing Ireland*, that, "every feature of Irish cultural life is seen to emanate from the colonial moment, while every other principle that might structure Irish cultural history, especially its modernity, is ignored" (Livesay and Murray 455). In respect to this statement, a project such as this study of Joyce is not trying to provide a conclusive study by offering a postcolonial reading of Joyce. Instead, it is hoped that the reader will use the postcolonial approach as one method of enriching our understanding of literature and culture without misconstruing the aim of the theory.

More serious still is another objection raised from the fringe of Irish studies, namely that postcolonial studies on the whole is a reductive formula that seeks to recreate a binary of colonial and postcolonial, and overly politicise reading while failing to illuminate the literature that this theory claims to investigate. This argument is taken up most directly by Roy Foster, who warns that postcolonial theory for Ireland has

> [r]esuscitated the ideas that progressivism and rationalism are innately imperialistic ideas. What some recent critics seem to opt for instead is an anti-developmentalist view, condemning any linear notion of history as whiggish in effect and colonialist by implication. (Foster xii)

While this study finds value in the same critics that Foster dismisses, this quote shows the vigilance necessary in postcolonial studies if this theory is to be grounded in literary study and to guard against turning postcolonial studies into a politically biased condemnation of British history.

The Irish role in postcolonial studies

Irish postcolonial status may have been overlooked because of the unique conditions of postcoloniality in Ireland. Kiberd explains that *The Empire Writes Back* "passes over the Irish case very swiftly, perhaps because the authors find these white Europeans too strange an instance to justify their sustained attention" (*Inventing* 5). Whatever the reasons for the Irish exclusion, not only can the case for Irish inclusion be made but it must be made. Irish writers who have been written into the English tradition have proved inspirational for the more recognised postcolonial writers. Examples of Irish inspiration include Achebe's *Things Fall Apart*, which was inspired by Yeats' "The Second Coming" (Walder 15), while J. M. Synge's *Playboy of the Western World* is not only reminiscent of Frantz Fanon's ideal of the decolonising text, but the play was later adapted by Mustafa Matura in Trinidadian as *The Playboy of the West Indies* (Kiberd, *Inventing* 185-188).

Perhaps the most fundamental of errors in terms of excluding Ireland's writers as postcolonial pioneers is the case in *The Empire Writes Back* where Wilson Harris' novel *Assent to Omai* (1970), is given credit for pioneering the use of the English language in a free way, apart from the tradition of binary bases, dismantling literature, language, history and time (Ashcroft, *Empire* 49-50). This summary not only undermines Harris' work, but also is factually incorrect, as the methods described above do not originate in the Caribbean, but in Europe, with the Irishman, James Joyce. The problem this distinction creates for the argument of *The Empire Writes Back* is a serious one. Essentially, the postcolonial writers of the Caribbean, Asia and Africa did not discover their own voice and perspective within the English language and literature, but merely copied a style that originates from a member of the centre, the United Kingdom's own James Joyce's and his novels *Ulysses* and *Finnegans Wake*. The importance here lies in admitting Joyce's role as outsider, maybe not in the same context as Achebe, Rusdie or Harris, but none the less, as a hybrid on the border between the coloniser and colony. Joyce's unique colonial perspective creates the opportunity for the other postcolonial nations to envision themselves as the ones in power of the English language, their art, and essentially their sovereignty.

Reading Ireland, and specially Joyce from the postcolonial angle, is essential not only for our wider understanding of postcolonial theory abroad, but locally as well. Lloyd explains:

> Under colonial conditions, there is no transcendence either of the political state or of culture. Liberal attempts that pretend to a Irish multiculturalism or models of the two (or more) traditions are simply dishonest to the extent that they ignore the asymmetrical and violent relations that have structured Ireland historically and contemporaneously. (*Cultural* 88)

Understanding that this may seem an extreme position to some, it is admitted that this is not the only approach to reading Joyce and Ireland. However, the postcolonial critical approach seems to highlight aspects of Joyce's writing and Irish culture and history that previously have gone underrepresented.

Joyce and Postcolonial Studies

In describing the complication of creating a version of Irish history that reconstructs the status of the nation's pre-colonial past, Gibbons writes:

> It was decidedly in the interest of native Irish historians to deny that Ireland was ever in a state of nature, and that it was culturally inscribed from the dawn of antiquity. The difficulty with this position was that the testimony on which it was based depended to a large extent on an oral heritage, and thus had to contend with a prejudice against popular memory, derived ultimately from the Protestant valorization of the written word at the expense of custom and tradition. (*Transformations* 153)

For one, this quotation again illustrates the trap of the colonised trying to compete on the same scale as the coloniser, which is always an unfair comparison, but one the colonised nation easily falls into on account of pride and nationalism. But furthermore, this quote should be read with Joyce's writing style in mind; consider the deconstruction of language and English literary tradition and expectations that is created over the course of his *oeuvre*. This point will be studied throughout this book, seeking to observe a writer that wants to undermine the control that the coloniser has over the written word, and in doing so give the novel and language itself to the colonised on equal terms with England.

In conclusion, Joyce studies have expanded to all reaches of literary and cultural theory, to the extent that Joyce can be made to represent conflicting sides of a given argument. Joseph O'Connor gives a humorous take on Joyce studies when he states:

> It was clear that you could make James Joyce say whatever you wanted him to say. He was like an academic version of a ventriloquist's dummy. Depending on whose hand was up him on which day, what he had to say would change substantially. (149)

O'Connor's point could be expanded by recognising that what Joyce has to say could change substantially as well, by what is left out of the reading. The decisive work to deal with Joyce and postcolonial theory, Cheng's *Joyce, Race, and Empire*, argues that Joyce has been too long regarded as an apolitical writer, to the point where he can be given a place in the English Literary Canon (2). By placing Joyce into the canon of English Literature, Cheng rhetorically asks,

> are we not, indeed, effectively muting and blunting (even ignoring) the power of the key motivations behind his writings, which were most frequently attempts to resist

1 Postcolonial Status 31

and defy the authorized centrality of canons, empires (especially England), and totalizing structures? (3)

The consequences of misreading Joyce as an English writer in relation to the postcolonial studies were examined earlier, however, in this passage Cheng further demonstrates that even an apolitical reading permits Joyce to be read as part of the English canon. Therefore reading the implied political message of Joyce's text both locates Joyce at the beginning of the postcolonial writing movement as well as opening Joyce to interpretations left aside by previous critics who assumed Joyce apolitical.

Chapter 2
The Articulation of Colonial Irish Identity in *Dubliners*: Homogeneity as Productive of Fantasy and Materialism instead of Idealism

To discuss Joyce's relation to colonialism is to consider the evolution of a career and philosophy divided appropriately enough by publication, ultimately developing towards the deconstruction of the English language, tradition and culture in *Finnegans Wake*. *Dubliners* provides the first subtle declaration for the initial need to decolonise. This essay begins by taking that mask of a capital or centre of paralysis and articulating the details of the lives of those characters, who could not at this point initiate the process of what Ngũgĩ wa Thiong'o might call the "decolonisation of the mind."

From "The Sisters" to "The Dead," *Dubliners* is a description of the problem of colonial life. Opposing one traditional narrative of postcolonial thought that life in the capital of a colonial state is "an altogether artificial life which is stuck on to the real, national life like a foreign body [and] ought to take up the least space as possible in the life of the nation, which is sacred and fundamental" (Fanon 151), Joyce finds value in describing the capital and its defeated components which represent the destroyed element of the national spirit. The characters of *Dubliners* are able to visualise another place, another life but are repeatedly defeated by either a disappointment in reality or disillusionment in terms of their inability to realise their aspirations. This underlying feature of the collection figures as the first challenge to any independent Irish identity, because action seems futile in the colonial setting where one is always subservient. These lives, that may seem dominated by Westminster and the Vatican as well as by their poverty and limited vision, may be gratefully oppressed, but the author describes the discontent that is unexplained. Although at no one point do the characters overtly express their grievances about colonial subjection, the frustrations are nearly realised in a crucial scene from "The Dead" in which Gabriel comes so close to explaining the difficulty that most characters experience:

> – O, to tell you the truth, retorted Gabriel suddenly, I'm sick of my own country, sick of it! – Why asked Miss Ivors. Gabriel did not answer for his retort had heated him. They had to go visiting together and as he had not answered her, Miss Ivors said warmly: – Of course you've no answer. (190)

Gabriel is unable to answer because he is torn between a desire to be a part of modern continental Europe as evidenced by his goloshes, associations with the conservative British press and interests in continental holidays, while simultaneously desiring to identify with the tradition that the "fathers have handed down to us and which we in turn must hand down to our descendants" (204). Gabriel, with perhaps more foresight than other characters, wishes Irish identity could expand to incorporate other cultures, and yet his feelings are in conflict with the narrow-mindedness of the colonial state. The binary reaction to colonial thinking is of course, nationalism. However nationalism as a cultural force tends to shun multiculturalism and openness, it also tends to prevent the creation of an Irish identity that would be more inclusive of continental and British values or opinions. Caught in-between the competing ideologies of nationalism and yet interested in the "other," the characters of *Dubliners* are in a sense paralysed.

The second postcolonial point of the collection lies in the value of the "sovereign." The references to money or the power of money in each story highlight the poverty of the times, but also stress the over-importance money has in social and moral values. This theme harks back to the betrayal of Parnell, where a favour or opinion can be bought at the price of dignity or even sovereignty. The emphasis on money in the collection describes a people who are individually looking for security while giving up on the national pursuit of long-term goals like national independence, political and economic sovereignty or more personally and perhaps importantly, their dignity, thus preventing any national unity by rejecting an idealistic sense of national philosophy while also redefining the national character as ruthless and self-interested.

Daydreaming Dubliners

When the young narrator of "The Sisters" softly says that strangely sounded word 'paralysis' to himself, he describes the central theme of the colonial city and its inhabitants. To read the collection as a protest that seeks to demonstrate the futility of life as the servant to the imperial power is possible, however, there is a sub-text that also counteracts that one-dimensional anti-colonial reading, that is, the lack of national pride. For instance, if the novel were to fit the prototype of the national decolonising text, then why not support rather than omit the Irish literary revival, the Irish language and Gaelic Athletic movements that were all overtly striving for national independence? I would suggest that this omission demarcates *Dubliners* as a unique anti-colonial text; it does not address the classic binary divide of Irish/British, or colonised/coloniser in any overt way. While *Dubliners* can be understood as a traditional appeal against imperialism in the more obvious portrayal of a city and nation in decline, it must also be read as a text that disrupts any nationalist sentiments of the nation as collectively struggling against imperialism. In this sense, the collection works to construct a decolonising theme while simultaneously deconstructing the nationalism most commonly involved with such a process of decolonisation.

Dubliners does not advise the nation to return to the past or identify with historic glories real or imagined, but instead illustrates a people who want to imagine new perspectives and interact with other cultures rather than narrowly refine their own. Gibbons has remarked that in Ireland's situation "[t]here was no need to go abroad to experience the 'multiple identities' of the diaspora valorized in post-colonial theory: the uncanny experience of being a stranger to oneself was already a feature of life back home" (*Transformations* 176).

This statement applies too well to *Dubliners* as although these characters initially think that there is nothing for them in Ireland, they eventually encounter something unexpected and seem to find some sort of uneasy distance within themselves in relation to their identities.

A new perspective for these characters comes in many forms, an old priest's stories, miching school, a middle-eastern quest, escape abroad, excitement with foreign friends, envisioning a conman's day, imagining escaping responsibility, fancying an unrealistic literary career, escaping reality, shrouding emotions and avoiding connections, imagining an Ireland with Parnell, exaggerating possible musical and societal success, conceiving religion as business or over-simplifying our identity and place in the world. While not thematically linked, each of these daydreams shows a desire to be more or have more than what is available in reality, and ultimately in each case the dream is disappointed. What makes this disillusionment original is that the failures are not presented as facts of life but as specific to Dublin's colonial paralysis.

Encounters with fantasy and reality

The reluctant Indians, including the narrator of "An Encounter," may not identify with the Wild West, but for a character who does not enjoy the subject of the impersonations, these imaginary games did "open doors of escape." Specifically, this need for escape for the narrator concerns "encountering" the outside world or otherness. The Native or contemporary American context of these fantasies allows the narrator to articulate a desire to see the world beyond his isolation: "[R]eal adventures, I reflected, do not happen to people who remain at home: they must be sought abroad" (12). The narrator does not have practical opportunities to seek adventure in America, but a day's miching could provide an opportunity to explore beyond his own neighbourhood.

However, the behaviour of the narrator and his friend Mahony in their interaction with a group of poor children continues the theme of Indian games, which of course inherently includes an imperial theme of another kind. Yet in this interaction the narrator and Mahony are not the wild Indians, but assert their superiority in the form of their strength and weaponry, now playing the role of the oppressors, aggressively pillaging, although eventually sparing, the poor "wild" Irish:

> He chased a crowd of ragged girls, brandishing his unloaded catapult and, when two ragged boys began, out of chivalry, to fling stones at us, he proposed that we should charge them. I objected that the boys were too small, and so we walked on, the ragged troop screaming after us: Swaddlers! Swaddlers! thinking that we were Protestants because Mahony, who was dark-complexioned, wore the silver badge of a cricket club in his cap. (14)

Remember that in the Indian games of escape organised by Joe Dillon, the mock battles strangely appear not to be the traditional game of Cowboys and Indians, but merely Indians and other Indians, as there is no mention of Cowboys and this is reinforced by the inclusion of the point that all battles ended with an Indian war victory dance. With the boys having left their neighbourhood, they have also left the role of Indian and it seems adopted the role of the imperial Cowboy, much in the same sense as soldiers in the American Calvary colonised the "Wild West" and likewise the British Army colonised the "Wild Irish."

Cheng has speculated that the narrator may not have identified with playing the Indian because the game links radicalised visions of Irishness with the Native Americans, "Irish were represented as similar to native American Indians in terms of a range of customs, personal habits, physical features, primitive wildness and resistance to civilizing" (84). Poignantly, this reading interprets the narrator as not wanting to be the radicalised other of British description, in other words the "wild Irishman," more than one who fancies himself as the powerful modern man. This identity desire for the narrator may mean identifying with an American detective but for the far more aggressive Mahony, it may mean identifying with the conquering colonial soldier. This interpretation shows the boys confused by their Irish identity. As the boys want to be a part of the system that rules the nation, they do not want to be the oppressed and this conscription on the part of British imperialism may be its most important victory.

Returning to the above quote, it should also be noted that in one of the rare occasions when the truly oppressed, raggedly poor are given voice they should call out the specific insult of 'Swaddlers.' These children have come to identify the Protestant outsider or the "dark skinned other" as a negative force, and for all of the insults they could have mustered, to identify dominating and aggressive behaviour with Protestantism at once seems both unfair and yet understandable.[6]

After this first encounter the two descend on the quays to see the international sailors. The narrator's desire here to escape to a foreign land is mirrored by Mahony who also feels:

> It would be right skit to run away to sea on one of those big ships and even I, looking at the high masts, saw, or imagined, the geography which had been scantily dosed to me at school gradually taking substance under my eyes. School and home seemed to recede from us and their influences upon us seemed to wane. (15)

This section describes how the narrator's desire is not isolated because Mahony also has a desire to be someone else and to go beyond the mono-culturalism of his neighbourhood and furthermore the nation.[7] The power of the boy's imagination should also be noted, the sight of the foreign ship alone is enough to give his energetic young mind grounds for conjuring up visual images of afar, and this near artistic, but still passive, state lets him distance

---

[6] Of course this is also an example of the tribalism that colonialism creates as described by Frantz Fanon in *The Wretched of the Earth*: "By its very structure, colonialism is separatist and regionalist. Colonialism does not simply state the existence of tribes: it also reinforces it and separates them" (74).

[7] It might be interesting to consider how this recession of mono-culturalism at the docks resembles the recession of nationalism in the University for Stephen in *Portrait*, where Stephen wonders why he feels so out of place in the corridor: "was the Jesuit house extraterritorial and was he walking among aliens? The Ireland of Tone and of Parnell seemed to have receded in space" (199). It is as if the colonial apparatus of state, religion and nationalism were a physical presence that could be avoided by crossing a border, such as a port or a Catholic school.

himself from his home and surroundings. It is this unusual condition that is not only common to the Narrator and Mahony but to the characters of other stories as well, most specifically perhaps in the conclusion of *Portrait* where Stephen writes:

> The spell of arms and voices: the white arms of roads, their promise of close embraces and the black arms of tall ships that stand against the mood their tale of distant nations. They are held out to say: We are alone. Come. And the voices say with them: We are your kinsmen. (275)

The correlation is that all of these characters have the ability to envision another space, but few have the courage to make something of the vision.

Other observations of the pair include the "little Jew with a bag" that rides with them in the ferryboat. This otherwise nondescript character does seem at least interesting as he is given an ethnic identity and a possession unlike the other passengers who were just "two labourers" who apparently, in their homogeneity, are not worth description. This point of interest is further exemplified when the boys spot a "Norwegian vessel" and the narrator wishes to examine "the foreign sailors to see had any of them green eyes [. . .]" ("Encounter" 15). The narrator's approach to foreigners foremost reflects his lack of interaction with any diversity. In this brief encounter with actual sailors, rather than those of his comics or imagination, he finds that his "confused notion" of sailors having green eyes is disappointed as "the sailor's eyes were blue and grey and even black" (15). Note how the eye colours are all types, all-inclusive, the misconceived stereotype turns out to be the opposite and extra stress seems to be given to "even black." Without trying to overemphasise this line, it seems it may be speaking about more than eye colour, the text may be demonstrating the existing diversity of the outside world in culture and race and, furthermore, it may be indicating that the confusion of the boys is based on their inaccurate and biased knowledge of the outside world, as it turns out that even black-eyed men could be sailors.

In briefly discussing the "encounter" with the "queer old josser," it might be noted that during his speech concerning "a nice warm whipping" the narrator notices when regarding the man's face, "the gaze of a pair of bottle-green eyes peering at me from under a twitching forehead. I turned my eyes away again" (19). In respect of the narrator's misconception of the eyes of foreign sailors, we find that this meeting with a fellow citizen turns out to be an awkward situation with a pervert. This reading interprets the encounter as being a disappointment; the foreign sailors are normal in appearance and the fellow Irishman is foreign in the sense that he is strange and unknowable. The narrator thus finds his conceptions at the beginning of the story shattered: the exotic other existing beyond the island nation can look as commonplace, the far more exotic and disturbing is the man of his own nation.

In conclusion, attention must be paid to the imagined names that the narrator uses for each of them: "In case he asks us for our names, I said, let you be Murphy and I'll be Smith" (18). Despite early attempts to imagine themselves as: Indians, detectives, conquerors, explorers, sailors or well-read students, by the conclusion the boys have taken the most common of Irish and Anglo surnames, hardly exotic or imaginative. This relatively minor aspect of the plot may read as an example of the inability to put imaginative possibilities to constructive ends; specifically, the boys are able to imagine in great detail minute aspects of fantasy, but when in need of a proper escape plan from the pervert they are only able to muster these simple realistic names.

Perhaps importantly, the narrator has taken the Anglo name Smith and in his desire to escape from the old man he calls out in "an accent of forced bravery" the name 'Murphy,' which in turn sends Mahony running across the field to the narrator "as if to bring me aid." Despite the comfort that Mahony attempts to provide, the narrator concludes, "in my heart I had always despised him a little" (20). In this reading, the final line would seem to show the narrator once again imagining himself as superior as when he was thinking he was too old to play Indian games, too bored to go to school, too strong to fight the ragged children or too smart to speak of literature with Mahony in the man's presence. Now he feels superior to Mahony although he is in the passive position, asking and now waiting for aid. In light of these circumstances the reader must wonder has he now imagined himself as the colonial power, the Anglo 'Smith' to his subservient 'Murphy'?

This reading presents us with Irish characters wanting to escape their position of subservience and boredom, however, despite the best ideas that their imaginations can muster, we have one character afraid to take part and the other two unable to find any freedom from their attempted adventures. Instead, their fantasy adventure is relocated in the most material of names, Murphy and Smith.

Self-isolation and the disillusioned fantasy world of James Duffy in "A Painful Case"

When the reader is first introduced to James Duffy she/he notices a similarity between his and the narrator's relation to the city in "An Encounter." This feeling specifically is Duffy's wish "to live as far as possible from the city of which he was a citizen" (103). Yet despite this sentiment towards Dublin, he does live in the outskirts of Chapelizod. Duffy's existence, like that of the previous characters, also lacks diversity as "his life rolled out evenly – an adventureless tale." Duffy, in this description would seem bored with his surroundings, and like the boy, he will seek adventure, but rather than a day of miching school, Duffy's adventure is a liaison with a married women.

Of course the significant difference between these two characters is their maturity. The narrator of "An Encounter" is bound to his family, but Duffy is an unattached adult who should be free to leave if he wishes and yet he is unable. The other difference between these characters is that the boy sees homogeneity in his surroundings and the lack of the other leads him to fantasy, whereas Duffy creates a life of controlled uniformity in order to maintain his esoteric intellectual games and prolong his solitary existence.

Duffy will never leave Dublin, because he had found ways of escaping his life's disappointments in his pseudo-intellectual escape from society. To begin with, Duffy constructs his surroundings in the same terms that he would like to imagine life as constructed, that is black, white and barren. He has a desire to live by what may be the ideals of his philosophical or political reading an anti-materialism linked with a pleasure in deprivation, this is borne out by the physical descriptions of his flat: "The lofty walls of his uncarpeted room were free from pictures." The room has "a black iron bedstead," "shelves of white wood," "white bedclothes," "a black and scarlet rug," "a white shaded lamp stood as the sole ornament of the mantelpiece" (103).

The passage quoted focuses on details that include colour. However the entire layout supports the cold and colourless existence of his chosen and created space. It is a life that lacks any sense of fullness, physically and also in intellectual activity.

The boys of "An Encounter" may have been fantasy-prone; however, Duffy is the epitome of a life spent trying to exist in his mind and ignore his body. To keep his life interesting Duffy's mind has devised a complex system of regarding himself in the third person:

> He lived at little distance from his body, regarding his own acts with doubtful side-glances. He had an odd autobiographical habit which led him to compose in his mind from time to time a short sentence about himself containing a subject in the third person and a predicate in the past tense. (104)

This description could be of the intellectual pursuits and disciplines that a writer might undertake to practice his craft, but we learn that Duffy quite rarely puts his intellectual work into action: it is far more for his own amusement or fantasy. In terms of his abilities to express his thoughts and experiences, we learn that despite ample free time only "a sentence was inscribed from time to time." Furthermore, this journal acts as a testament to his lack of expression, as it is stored in a desk with an odour of "an over-ripe apple which might have been left there and forgotten" (104). These images suggest what may have been a powerful mind and certainly imagination that has been left to go to rot. Unable to create a productive end for his abilities, Duffy uses this surplus merely to construct a life of isolation from others as well as for himself.

Later in the story it will be asked of Duffy, "why did he not write out his thoughts." To which he for once emotionally, if not in a bit of a rehearsed phrasing, protests: "For what, he asked her, with careful scorn. To compete with phrasemongers, incapable of thinking consecutively for sixty seconds? To submit himself to the criticisms of an obtuse middle class which entrusted its morality to policemen and its fine arts to impresarios?" (107).

The phrase "careful scorn" seems to alert the reader to the fact that Duffy must have some insecurities about his lack of expression and the carefully constructed witticism concerning art and morality would lead the reader to believe that these could have been former entries in his creative papers and this self-conscious joking would seem to make something of a "phrasemonger" of Duffy himself. Furthermore, his jibe about not thinking consecutively should be contrasted with the fact that he rarely records a single sentence, with no mention of anything more. This sensitive subject shows that the one area in which Duffy would like to profess his competence, that is his intellect that lets him pride himself over others, is in fact a mockery. Instead, Duffy has never expressed his thoughts, and uses his intellectual capabilities only for building his fantasy realm for his detached lifestyle.

It is stated that Mr. Duffy, "abhorred anything which betokened physical or mental disorder" (104). Possibly this abhorrence may be based on the delicate constructs of a life composed to provide total disconnection from the ties of humanity. However, this construct is threatened when Duffy makes a connection with Emily Sinico. For Duffy, of whom it is stated that he "had neither companions nor friends, church nor creed," it seems this interaction will be positive, but from the first line that Sinico speaks to him, he treats the relationship as a performance rather than friendship. Sitting next to Duffy, Sinico remarks on the poor attendance: "It's so hard on people to have to sing to empty benches" (105). Duffy seems to take this comment not only as an opportunity to begin a conversation and eventually a friendship, but also as an invitation to be her entertainer. In other words, he fantasises himself as being the singer so unfortunate to have to sing to empty benches.

Now, like the singer in the concert hall, Duffy has what he feels he has been missing in life, an audience for his thoughts in Mrs. Sinico.

For her part, Sinico is perfect for him because, "she listened to all." It is in her dedication to him that he feels her "like a warm soil about an exotic;" furthermore, Duffy "thought that in her eyes he would ascend to an angelical stature." Both examples, which are full of self-conscious flattery, show Duffy viewing himself from a third person perspective, which should question any of his claims that this relationship could be the "union" he describes. Her role is generally passive listening, but the narrator intervenes, "she became his confessor." This is an important distinction for a man who was noted as having neither church nor creed earlier and it also foreshadows the fact that a listener is a part of the conversation, as Sinico will want to take part in the discussion later.

Before Sinico's desire to make the connection that Duffy's conversations seem to be offering is realised, it is necessary to recall the socialist party meetings that Duffy had attended. Duffy's initial attraction to the group may have been based on his philosophical interests or more likely the fact that his presence at such meetings would make him feel "himself a unique figure amidst a score of sober workmen." But essentially he never makes a connection with the other members because "he felt that they were hard-featured realists and that they resented an exactitude which was the product of a leisure not within their reach" (107). This quotation is at once another example of his superiority complex and his inability to connect with others because his isolated world view conflicts with the world of action, the reality with which his fellow socialists are engaged.

In accordance with this history of disconnection from ideals and reality, we read that Duffy is likewise able to encourage Mrs.

Sinico with his visits, companionship and conversation as he had done with the socialists. But the relationship takes on a real meaning when "Mrs. Sinico caught up his hand passionately and pressed it to her cheek": he finds himself again "surprised" and "disillusioned." Duffy is able to imagine himself a socialist or Sinico as his "soul's companion," but the reality of taking on the commitment to something, someone else, is unrealisable because of his self-constructed fantasy realm that would be lost in leaving his isolation for connection with others in reality.

The previously studied characters from "An Encounter" may have wanted escape and freedom, but they were trapped in the reality of childhood, whereas Duffy wants the same things as the children but his fantasy is repressed and this repression figures as an analogy for a nation that may be able to imagine change but is unwilling to embrace an opportunity when it is offered.

Sovereign State

Momentary images of the "ragged" poor scatter *Dubliners*. These portrayals of the unfortunate are brief and these characters are almost never given a voice. Yet their inclusion in *Dubliners* highlights the division in Irish society considering the overall poverty of almost all characters. However, poverty in Ireland when compared to the economic strength of the colonial powers, further highlights Irish colonial stature. Demonstrating this occurrence where the impoverished Irish are contrasted to the colonial masters is the story "After the Race," where the reader is reminded of this disparity of wealth and power: "Sightseers had gathered in clumps to watch the cars careering homeward and through this channel of poverty and inaction the Continent sped its wealth and industry. Now and again the clumps of people raised the cheer of the gratefully oppressed" (35).

This intricate description portrays the Irish as exploited outsiders, passively watching the colonial powers flex their affluence and superiority. In fact, the term "careering" brilliantly describes the movement and pace of the cars, but of course the word's other meaning would allude to a vocation or a profession, which then brings about an image of the continentals making a livelihood out of the colonial enterprise at the expense of the colonised Irish.

The word choice in this passage is not only poetic in terms of the "careering" double-entendre, but one also notices the contrast in the shape of the sightseers who are merely "clumps," formless masses rather than individuals, and the sleek design of the speeding race cars. The oppressed in this picture cheer on the continentals for what they have achieved, wealth and power, but the Irish crowds do not take issue with the colonial power's wealth and industry being achieved through the exploitation of Ireland and other colonial nations. Essentially, the colonial subjects have come to perceive the colonial power's wealth and industry as attractive, something that these oppressed masses are happy to applaud from a spectator's position even as they are used as a catalyst and resource for their oppressor.

This treatment would seem to agree with the traditional postcolonial narrative that could describe colonial subjection as leading to poverty, lowered self-esteem and eventually a manipulation of the values that belonged to the nation before colonialism. While these aforementioned aspects may be exhibited in *Dubliners*, the inability of these "clumps" to show disdain at such a display of affluence and exploitation in the face of their poverty complicates a postcolonial interpretation. These colonial Irish subjects are actually "grateful" for the oppression, some characters will even strive to learn from the oppressor and profit in the exploitation of their own people. As Fanon notes, "The colonized man is an envious man. [T]here is no native who does not dream at least once a day of setting himself up in the settler's place" (30). Although Fanon may have overstated the idea, his point is valid in that some of the Dubliners would prefer to profit like the coloniser, rather than be a part of the clump.

Few mentions outside that of the narrator's voice draw attention to the essential postcolonial problem of oppression. In this regard, *Dubliners* presents a traditional decolonisation message about the disparity of the masses while simultaneously giving an anti-nationalist and condemnatory vision of Irish complacency and willingness to turncoat. Macauley's programmatic *Minute on Indian Education*, for example, makes this point from the colonial perspective, in its attempt to create a "class of persons, Indian in blood and colour, but English in taste, in opinions, in morals, and in intellect" (430), a perspective which seems to rule out any notion of an Indian having either indigenous or hybrid qualities of taste, opinions, morals or intellect.

This reading emphasises that "terrible game" illustrated in "After the Race" whereby the colonial subject wants to be proverbially dealt in to the colonial power's game of cards. In this story, Doyle feels "the buried zeal of his father wake to life within him" (39). That zeal is a nationalistic reaction on the part of the Irishman when discussing politics with the English Routh, as well as the Frenchmen Ségouin and Rivière, who are the representatives of colonial power. This nationalistic zeal lies buried because of Doyle's desire to please his oppressors and prosper for himself rather than support an idealistic notion that might be of greater benefit for the whole of his nation. Doyle's case is not singular, even this character's father is an example of a man who

> had begun life as an advanced Nationalist, [but] had modified his views early. He had made his money as a butcher in Kingstown [. . .]. He had also been fortunate enough to secure some of the police contracts and in the end he had become rich enough to be alluded to in the Dublin newspapers as a merchant prince. (36)

The father significantly changes his politics for his business's sake, switching from the distinction of "advanced" nationalist to making a fortune selling to the police, an apparatus of colonial oppression. Fanon has noted that for some "nationalisation quite simply means the transfer into native hands of those unfair advantages which are legacy of the colonial period" (122). In other words, this nationalist is happy to assume the privilege of power without accounting for his role in maintaining the colonial status quo. Furthermore, the note of his image as "merchant prince" conjures ideas of an autonomous individual; hardly fitting with the self-styled image of unified citizens that Irish nationalism espouses.

The colonised desire to have the coloniser's wealth and power is a feature that contributes to the loss of the national identity. As the Irish representative Doyle learns, "he would lose," the colonial subject will never be able to compete in the same game as the colonial master.[8] Many of *Dubliners'* characters make attempts to

---

[8] Fanon writes: "The well-being and the progress of Europe have been built up with the sweat and the dead bodies of Negroes, Arabs, Indians, and the yellow races" (76). The colonised start with a disadvantage upon independence as they cannot create themselves with the same aid of colonisation that fattened Europe. Here the end of the game in "After the Race" deconstructs the fantasy of having parity of esteem with the coloniser by Doyle's losses in the game: "It was a terrible game. [. . .] Jimmy understood that the game lay between Routh and Ségouin. [. . .] Jimmy was excited too; he would lose of course.

better themselves at the expense of others, without regard for the greater good. This backstabbing on the part of the Irish may first read as not contributing to a decolonising narrative, but the reason for this sub-plot is to show the effects of colonialism in its ability to divide the people and change the national goals and aspirations. By looking at some examples of this undercurrent in the collection, the reader finds the Irish taking their coloniser's values to their own lives with the consequence of painting an unflattering picture of the colonial Irish character.

One gallant learns from another

Although an Irishman, Corley of "Two Gallants" supports the English colonial campaign by profiting at the expense of fellow Irish. From the first mention of Corley, the reader notices this character near Rutland Square, the site of an Orange Order Lodge which makes a connection, however subtly, with English political power and oppression. However, this is not the only occurrence of Corley's associations and joint profiting with the coloniser. It is later noted that "Corley was the son of an inspector of police and he had inherited his father's frame and gait" ("Two Gallants" 45). This quote has two points for illustration, for one, the father's link to the police is another example of an Irishman working for a colonial system that serves to control the Irish for the benefit of English rule. Secondly, the son has inherited a likeness to his father; the reader may picture Corley as not only as physically like his fa-

---

How much had he written away?" (41). Furthermore, as Jimmy is realising his loss and the English and French advantage the story concludes with the announcement of "Daybreak, gentlemen!" It is as if this metaphorical description of nationhood depicts Ireland, Hungary and the United States with the inherited disadvantages of losing out on the spoils of colonialism.

ther but also as ideologically similar because of the attention that is given to the "gait," that style of stride that the narrator observes in Corley. This subtle aspect of word choice foreshadows the line that describes Corley's "easy pace and the solid sound of his boots had something of the conqueror in them" ("Two Gallants" 49). This notion of "something of the conqueror" is essential to the postcolonial reading of the collection because Corley is a character who is not a direct symbol of the empire, but nonetheless figures as someone who works against Irish nationalist ideas in favour of developing a career out of self-advancement through the exploitation of the colonised Irish. Corley in this sense is a micro-coloniser mimicking England's macro-colonisation.

This role is passed from father to son, as it had been done previously in "After the Race." Further illustrating Corley's disreputable approach to life is his first source of income, namely that of police informer as Corley was "often to be seen walking with policemen in plain clothes, talking earnestly" ("Two Gallants" 45). Terence Brown notes on this line, "the spy or informer of course plays an ignominious role in the history of Irish rebellion" (introduction 260-261). Brown's comment further supports the idea that Corley figures as a treacherous Irishman serving the enemy of Irish unity and liberation for the sake of his own profit. However, these associations with the coloniser and displays of profiteering on Corley's account are mild when compared to his second source of income.

Although Corley is not the central character of "Two Gallants" his rendezvous with a housekeeper is the driving action of the story. Consistently, this assignation, like almost all other relationships in the collection, has nothing to do with love. For Corley, women are a means of exploitation, an opportunity to take the benefits of their work for the sake of his own security and advancement. Corley's advice on the subject of women and dating is simply, "There's nothing to touch a good slavey, he affirmed. Take my tip of it." Essentially, Corley has incorporated a method for advancement based on colonial oppression, as he seeks to take advantage of his fellow oppressed citizen through the same systematic course that the coloniser has used to oppress him. He labels her a 'slavey,' a word that is slang for her housekeeping job, but ironically may be interpreted as not only a slave to her employers but to Corley as well in her willingness to provide Corley with money that she had earned.

Corley's attitude towards women must have developed over time as illustrated in his sentimental speech to Lenehan about how he used to date respectable girls. But for Corley these relationships were essentially unprofitable: "I used to take them out, man, on the tram somewhere and pay the tram or take them to a band or a play at the theatre or buy them chocolate and sweets or something that way. [. . .] And damn the thing I ever got out of it [. . .]" (46).

Corley's attitude towards women has matured from his earlier gentlemanly ways, which for him accomplished few of the goals that he now strives for in relationships, but this speech of "convincing tone" presents a character who certainly at one time would have identified with a more romantic or even humane vision of relationships. Corley's conversion of attitude is significant for understanding the design of this theoretical reading, for as Corley has learned the ways of the coloniser and imposed his own domination upon others, so will Lenehan attempt to learn the ways of the coloniser from Corley.

Although Corley may conquer the housekeeper, the character that loses the most dignity is Lenehan. Lenehan may not be a wholly likable individual, but he is a harmless one who makes his way as a "sporting vagrant armed with a vast stock of stories, limericks and riddles. [. . .] No one knew how he achieved the stern task of living [. . .]" (44). This description is like the caricature of a "Shauneen" who makes his living in the fawning and toadying of his conquering superiors. But Lenehan with his insincere personality, while certainly out for self-survival and without much thought for self-respect, acts in a way that does not interfere with the well-being of others. But Lenehan is not such a simple caricature, as he recognises a void in his life and this makes him

> feel keenly his own poverty of purse and spirit. He was tired of knocking about of pulling the devil by the tail, of shifts and intrigues. He would be thirty-one in November. Would he never get a good job? Would he never have a home of his own? [. . .] He might yet be able to settle down in some snug corner and live happily if he could only come across some good simple-minded girl with a little of the ready. (52)

These thoughts would seem to exemplify a man who now sees his faults and wants to make a change. Ironically, Lenehan finds fault in the fact that he is not scheming and chancing enough. He strangely does not understand that the poverty he encounters, the lack of good job, a home and a good relationship are exactly because of his "pulling of the devil's tail."

As Lenehan studies Corley he sees the success that he desires made possible with the skills that he believes he already possesses. Lenehan had used his speaking ability for smaller schemes, but while walking around contemplating Corley's more scandalous exploits, he becomes disheartened about his talents: "He found trivial all that was meant to charm him and did not answer the glances which invited him to be bold. He knew that he would have to speak a great deal, to invent and to amuse, and his brain and throat were too dry for such a task" (50).

This combination makes Lenehan want to change his attitude towards life from that of a mere freeloader to that of an aggressive dominator. In order to make the transformation he takes Corley's rendezvous as a case study in exploitation. The investigation begins by asking many questions, "Where did you pick her up, Corley?" (44). When Corley begins to unfold his plot of taking some money from the housekeeper, Lenehan becomes interested in the detail and has trouble believing such a scam can be achieved:

> – Well… tell me Corley, I suppose you'll be able to pull it off all right, eh?
>
> Corley closed one eye expressively as an answer.
>
> – Is she game for that? asked Lenehan dubiously. You can never know women.
>
> [. . .]
>
> – But tell me, said Lenehan again, are you sure you can bring it off all right? You know it's a ticklish job. They're damn close on that point. Eh… ? What? (46-47)

This passage illustrates both Corley's stated experience and willingness in such matters as well as Lenehan's interest and awe of the greater schemer's ability. Lenehan's respect is further expressed when he complements Corley's estimation that a housekeeper is the best sucker by stating, "By one who has tried them all" (46). By this point, Lenehan has begun to believe that Corley might succeed and when an opportunity arrives to see the master and the soon to be exploited girl, Lenehan demands access: "Let's have a squint at her, Corley [. . .]. Damn it! [. . .] I don't want an introduction. All I want is to have a look at her. I'm not going to eat her" (48). This rare outward show of force by Lenehan shows his growing desire to learn Corley's ways, to be the one with control rather than the one subjected.

Significantly, as in previous stories that focused on the daydreaming of characters which keeps them from accomplishing their desires, so too does Lenehan, at least initially, spend more time considering the possibility of an exploitive affair than on pursuing one. While enjoying his peas and ginger beer lunch, Lenehan idles and "sat for some time thinking of Corley's adventure. In his imagination he beheld the pair of lovers walking along some dark road" (51). Lenehan continues in his daydreaming ways for some time only to be interrupted by some acquaintances but soon enough, "his mind became active again. He wondered had Corley managed it successfully" (53). While this pensiveness would seem to follow the course of the previous characters studied above, the difference lies in the previously outlined argument for Lenehan's desire to learn Corley's exploitive ways.

Lenehan has waited the entire evening to find the results of Corley's exploits and when Corley's date/work is finished, Lenehan demands of him the outcome. Although ignored at first by Corley, Lenehan eventually initiates a telling response from his better: "Can't you tell us? he said. Did you try her? Corley halted at the first lamp and stared grimly before him. Then with a grave gesture he extended a hand towards the light and, smiling, opened it slowly to the gaze of his disciple. A small gold coin shone in the palm" (54-55).

In effect, describing Lenehan as "his disciple" fuels this reading more than any other example. The word 'disciple,' whether understood as a follower or a student of the master has the same effect on this reading, that is that the story follows the development of Lenehan's desire to be more like or to learn from Corley. Furthermore, as demonstrated above, Corley has learned his tricks of exploitation in a metaphorical way from the empire. In this postcolonial study the broad message is that the destruction of colonialism is not limited to native cultural erosion, but in the change of cultural values to those of the oppressor. In this case, that lesson sees the development of a ruthless lust for money, the loss of cultural unity and a change in the attributes that are found admirable in Irish culture. To put this idea in a theoretical context, consider Louis Althusser's concept of Ideological State Apparatuses (ISAs) and Repressive State Apparatuses (RSAs). In Althusser's familiar Marxian explanation, the State maintains its power by controlling its citizens through these two methods: RSAs which are the tools of violent or physical control, namely "the Government, the administration, the Army, the Police, the Courts, the Prisons," the other method is the ISAs, such as the church, the family, the school, the political party (136-137). Taking Althusser into account, Lenehan can be read as influenced by the RSA of British colonialism coupled with the ISA of Corley's corrupting influence.

Corresponding Characters: Lenehan and Farrington

Corley's preying on the innocent housekeeper might have been the most despicable act of the collection if it was not for Farrington, the abhorrent character of "Counterparts." Farrington however, until he assails his young son so cruelly in the story's final action, is portrayed sympathetically. Although like Lenehan, Farrington lives on the fringe of respectability, the difference being that his ostracism is not because of a thinly veiled desire to cheat or use others but because of his reluctance to give in to the hierarchical structures about him. Farrington's character is notable because of his desire to resist incorporation into his company's system, his unique use of fantasy compared to the other characters of *Dubliners* and his demonstrations of strength and lack of technique.

From one perspective, Farrington is a rebel personality. "Counterparts" effectively gives the reader the other extreme of Lenehan and Corley, in that Farrington initially tries to resist authority. Farrington's desire to resist authority is repeatedly shown in his subtle acts of subversion on the job and his reluctance to fit into the company's working structure.

Some of Farrington's behaviour may be explained by alcoholism, but his attitude towards his boss also reads as a metaphor for the colonial subject unwillingly working for the foreign master. In this analogy, the Northern-Irish, Unionist and Protestant, Mr. Alleyne, employs and dominates the Catholic-Irish Farrington. The political implications ensue as these binary identities also assume their respective power-roles with Alleyne, the aggressive controlling boss of the Irishman. Instead of what would appear to be purely a battle for power, what occurs here is a contractual discourse wherein power is codified in hierarchical structures, and where physical power is no longer part of the equation.

Farrington has a poor reputation in Alleyne's company due to his inability to complete assignments. On account of this inability, Alleyne is forced to reprimand Farrington for his lack of production but this motivational speech shows little effect as the narrator notices Farrington "took up his pen and dipped it in the ink but he continued to stare stupidly at the last words he had written" (84). Although the reader may wish to sympathise with Farrington because of the way his boss reproaches him, the strength of the word choice "stupidly" signifies the boss's need to voice such criticism at an employee unwilling to work. However, what may seem like plain idling to the boss actually is a complicated internal struggle for Farrington, who does not care about the necessity of getting the job done for Alleyne's sake, but often uses his work time to daydream, which undermines the boss.

In the opening scene, which presents the furious working conditions as a copywriter at Crosbie & Alleyne, the reader finds Farrington a tired and harassed employee. Yet despite all of the responsibility and pressure placed on Farrington he chooses to daydream and avoid work. Farrington's lack of productivity however is not because he lacks the intelligence to understand his responsibilities; in fact, Farrington is clever enough to devise ways of evading his responsibility. After finding himself unable to perform, Farrington plans to leave the building, but under the watchful eye of a fellow employee he is obliged to hide his intentions by calling out to the clerk: "It's all right, Mr Shelley, said the man, pointing with his finger to indicate the objective of his journey," which would be understood to be a trip to the men's room. However, in the following paragraph, Farrington's intentions are revealed:

> The chief clerk glanced at the hat-rack but, seeing the row complete, offered no remark. As soon as he was on the landing the man pulled a shepherd's plaid cap out of his pocket, put it on his head and ran quickly down the rickety stairs. From the street door he walked on furtively on the inner side of the path towards the corner and all at once dived into a doorway. He was now safe in the dark snug of O'Neill's shop, and, filling up the little window that looked into the bar with his inflamed face, the colour of dark wine or dark meat, he called out:

– Here, Pat, give us a g.p.. like a good fellow. ("Counterparts" 84)

This passage begins by describing the regularity and ingenuity of Farrington's ability to dodge work. By literally having a trick up his sleeve, Farrington deceives the clerk and then secretively slides down the street and into a pub with which he is familiar. Farrington then hurriedly "drank it at a gulp and asked for a caraway seed" ("Counterparts" 84). The lack of enjoyment from the drink and the taking of caraway seed to hide the scent of alcohol on his breath further demonstrate Farrington's intentions to subvert his employers. Upon return to the office, the clerk asks in annoyance where Farrington has been, to which the clerk replies, "I know that game [. . .]. Five times in one day is a little bit…" (85). This statement, and the actions of the story thus far illustrated, portray Farrington as competent enough to fulfil his job, but rather than use this energy to do his work he devises ways of wasting time and escaping from the dreary reality of work in a more successful, but ultimately more damaging manner than the previously discussed characters.

After leaving the office physically to evade work, Farrington will further avoid his copy by daydreaming at his desk. Caught in his truancy and with a head still confused by the glass of porter taken, Farrington returns to find that the copy Alleyne wants immediately will not be achievable and the frustration of now not having the time to finish only instigates more time wasting as immediately after Farrington's returning to his work the narrator describes how "[t]he dark damp night was coming and he longed to spend it in the bars, drinking with his friends [. . .]. [H]is mind wandered away to the glare and rattle of the public-house. It was a night for hot punches" (85-86). These fantasies of the pub displace anxiety over the day's wasted work and the trouble that may be caused on account of his irresponsibility. However, when a handwriting error leaves Farrington with a ruined sheet, we see the violent side of this character for the first time: "Blast it! He couldn't finish it in time. He longed to execrate aloud, to bring his fist down on something violently" (86). At first it seems that Farrington is taking the responsibility upon himself for having ruined the copy, but his desire to "execrate" seems far more likely to indicate that he feels an injustice has been done to him, rather than take the blame himself. Furthermore, Farrington wants to vent this frustration by hitting something, in the narrator's words with "violence." Farrington's true weakness is exposed here, as writing out the copy again or quitting the job that is causing this frustration can solve his problem, but he instead lets the setback affect him emotionally and favours using what he sees as his superior physical strength in these problems rather than rationalise a solution.

With the deadline arrived, Farrington leaves his desk for Alleyne's office and hopes "Mr. Alleyne would not discover that the last two letters were missing" (85). However, Farrington is losing control of his passion, "the barometer of his emotional nature was set for a spell of riot" (86). After this ominous forecast, the inevitable happens as the boss approaches having learned of the incomplete copy being submitted. Alleyne interrupts Farrington who is thinking of who might lend him money and where he might meet his friends for the evening, when the narrator notices "his imagination had so abstracted him that his name was called twice before he answered" (86). Being caught off guard further confuses Farrington and he literally stands up to Alleyne but says nothing while Alleyne "began a tirade of abuse." Alleyne's reprimand is so powerful that it inspires further anger from Farrington: "the man could hardly restrain his fist from descending upon the head of the manikin before him" (87). Similarly to his frustration with the copy error, Farrington wants to use his physical superiority to respond to his agitator. But showing surprising restraint, even as Alleyne mocks Farrington and his speech, he finds that words serve as the best revenge with a humorous response to Alleyne's question, "Do you think me an utter fool?," to which Farrington responds, 'I don't think, sir, [. . .] that that's a fair question to put to me" (87). By essentially telling Alleyne that he is in fact the fool, which sends his boss into a vile rage, Farrington has won the confrontation even if it is at the cost of the job. But in effect, Farrington did not have to use violence to win the exchange, with cool poise he outwits Alleyne and in doing so Farrington expresses his opinion and endears himself to the others who dislike Alleyne. In Farrington's comeback, the story presents its positive crescendo, which ebbs during the night of drinking.

Fantasy plays a different role in consideration of Farrington's self image as the second half of the story concerns his social life. Like the previously studied characters of "An Encounter" and "A Painful Case," Farrington wants to escape reality and his life. The difference in "Counterparts" is, however, the self-destructive nature of Farrington's fantasy, as while physically trying to engage with others, he finds himself unable to do so and therefore he creates fantasies concerning his frustration of not being able to control his surroundings.

Farrington's self-image is based on his physical strength. He judges Alleyne on several occasions for his diminutive stature and thinks of his ability to literally crush his boss. As illustrated above, Farrington wishes to use his physical strength to solve all problems, but he also exaggerates his own strength. For example, when frustration arises in the office the narrator notices, "He felt strong enough to clear out the whole office single-handed. His body ached to do something, to rush out and revel in violence" (86). This description portrays Farrington as "feeling" as if he has the power of a giant, a feeling that he justifies by attributing it to his body as if he has no control over it or his emotions. After leaving work Farrington "felt his great body again aching for the comfort of the public-house" (88). These repeated feelings of the body's control over the individual serve as demonstrations of Farrington's self-image of being an immensely physically powerful man, with the regret that he has not the ability to control himself.

Given his self-image it comes as little surprise that his encounter with the opposite sex at the pub is completely physical in nature. Repeated descriptions of Farrington's "dirty eyes" complement the scene as his glance "wandered at every moment in the direction of one of the young women" (91). Farrington takes careful notice of one woman's physical appearance and admires her clothing, her eyes, her expression and her "plump arm," but their contact is limited to a brief meeting of their eyes and her apology upon bumping into him. Characteristically, Farrington becomes enraged that his own physical attributes were not enough in this case to attract further attention from the woman. His dismay at her leaving forces another stereotypical response, as he was "so angry that he lost count of the conversation of his friends" (91). He also admits, "His heart swelled with fury and, when he thought of the woman in the big hat who had brushed against him and said *Pardon!* his fury nearly choked him" (93). The lesson Farrington might have learned from the office should have been that speaking up would have been the best option in this situation, but he instead solely relies on his physical presence to do the work. Furthermore, this self-image of strongman is about to be tested.

Unable to dominate the working institution or this woman with his physical strength Farrington is given an opportunity to use his strength for its seemingly most straightforward use: "When Paddy Leonard called him he found that they were talking about feats of strength. Weathers was showing his biceps muscle to the company and boasting so much that the other two had called on Farrington to uphold the national honour" (91-2).

This passage needs examining on several levels. For one, Farrington's one asset throughout the story has been his reliance on his physical power over others, an arm wrestling contest would seem to be the most straightforward opportunity to display his dominance. However, Weathers will make for exceptionally significant competition because Farrington personally dislikes Weathers, feeling envy for his life as an artist, which seems glamorous compared to Farrington's own existence. This jealousy is compounded with Paddy Leonard's demand for Farrington "to uphold the national honour."

The arm wrestling scene provides reminders of the binary of Irish and Northern Irish in the work place, but this confrontation concludes differently as Irish Farrington wrestles the Englishman. However, while the former encounter was about intelligence, this meeting would seem to be about strength, giving Farrington the advantage. Conversely, the narrator informs us that "[a]fter about thirty seconds Weathers brought his opponent's hand slowly down to the table. Farrington's dark wine-coloured face flushed darker still with anger and humiliation at having been defeated by such a stripling" (92).

Weathers is smaller, perhaps only a stripling, but his training as an acrobat has given him the technique to win the match. Farrington resorts to accusing Weathers of unfair play, but clearly lacks the ability to win and therefore "he had lost his reputation as a strong man, having been defeated twice by a mere boy" (93). Farrington must now reconsider his self-image as his defining quality is made out to be a fantasy of his imagination.

At the conclusion of the story, Farrington returns home defeated, not only from a bad day at work, a failed romance, and an arm wrestling match, but also in his desire to rebel against those injustices. Farrington will now exemplify Fanon's claim that "the development of violence among the colonised people will be proportionate to the violence exercised by the threatened colonial regime" (69). This means that compounding the violent trauma of colonialism with a faltering colonial system creates a need for violence, though this is not necessarily a positive release from the colonised experience. When Farrington finds the slightest reason to dominate, he takes the opportunity by mocking his son's excuse for his mother, "*At the chapel. At the chapel, if you please!*" (94). Of course Farrington is only mimicking the events of earlier in the day when Alleyne had mocked him, "– But Mr Shelley said, sir..." (83). Essentially, Farrington has incorporated his oppressor's mentality and now chooses to mimic the boss, not only in copying his papers, but also in copying Alleyne's aggressive style of coercion. Farrington then proceeds to use his physical strength to beat the child. This displacement of violence against the colonial power onto those less able to defend themselves is an allegory of the self-destructive forces that allow the colonial power to achieve hegemony.

The perversely comic ending has Farrington using the wrong method, violence rather than words, against the wrong target, his child rather than his oppressors, as his aim for vengeance. His day's work, and the achievement of the good comeback to the boss, and the night out's hard lesson of the mind being a superior tool than the body, should have taught Farrington something. But the only lesson learned is the lesson of oppression taught by Alleyne as Farrington uses his body to hurt the one person that means him good will.

To conclude this chapter, we may read *Dubliners* as presenting a picture of Irish consciousness that is trapped between desires to be free of paralysis and conversely a desire to have the coloniser's power. In both cases, the desires go unarticulated by the characters, and are only occasionally recognised by the narrator. Continuing this study, the following text will begin to devote greater attention to this problem of colonial Irish identity.

Chapter 3
The Evolution of Stephen Dedalus and Irish Identity:
The Allegory of Personal and National Liberation in *A Portrait of the Artist as a Young Man* and *Stephen Hero*

The previous chapter's reading has attempted to interpret *Dubliners* as an allegory for the identity question of pre-independence Ireland, in that the characters are unable to realise their desires because of the lack of opportunity for constructive ends combined with the influence of oppression, so that the collection does not provide a character capable of change, of developing independently or thinking autonomously for constructive conclusions. However, in *A Portrait of the Artist as a Young Man* and *Stephen Hero*, the reader finds Stephen Dedalus.[9] Stephen is different from the previous Joycean characters in terms of his relation to his surroundings, for instance, Mr. Doyle of "A Painful Case" may feel as if he is an exotic plant, but Stephen far more fits the description of an exotic in his society. Importantly, Stephen comes to feel this metaphorical Irish soil around him as restricting, isolated and colonised. Stephen is the first character in Joycean writing to seize control of his situation, and therefore he figures as being particularly important in the allegory of Irish identity as the instance of genius or epiphany by imagining himself outside of the confines

---

[9] John Paul Riquelme has illustrated that the Stephens of *Ulysses*, *Portrait* and *Stephen Hero* are all different Stephens and are further complicated by the critical desire to read Joyce as Stephen (103-104). Although this thesis has tried to avoid the character/ narrator/author discussion that Joyce studies often embraces; it seems less problematic for this argument to read these Stephens as interrelated, while admitting that they are different. Those differences are analysed when it affects this reading and influences any interpretation of colonial Irish identity within the Joycean oeuvre.

of nationalism and oppression to become an independent person or in terms of the analogy, an independent nation.

It should perhaps first be noted that Stephen's Dublin is not foreign to the representation of the city in *Dubliners*, as may be evidenced by the following brief description: "A young lady was standing on the steps of the one of those brown brick houses which seem the very incarnations of Irish paralysis" (*Stephen* 188). This passage combines the association-laden images of *Dubliners* that may figure as evidence of the ongoing situation: for example, references back to the word paralysis, from 'The Sisters', the brown brick houses that figured as faces of the same city in 'Eveline', and this image of the young women, perhaps representing the most repressed class of *Dubliners*.

More important than the symbolic image of the city is that the comparison to *Dubliners* continues in the characters surrounding Stephen as his family members and friends suffer similar fates as the previously studied characters. For instance, Stephen's mother voices the familiar desire to have something unavailable, to be somewhere or someone she is not: "But sometimes – not that I grumble at the lot Almighty God has given me and I have more or less a happy life with your father – but sometimes I feel that I want to leave this actual life and enter another – for a time" (*Stephen* 80). Likewise Stephen's father can be identified with those characters for whom fantasy plays a more significant role in self-perception than reality as exampled by this section:

> Stephen's father was quite capable of talking himself into believing what he knew to be untrue [. . .] Mr. Dedalus had been accustomed to regard himself as the centre of a little world, the darling of a little society. This position he still strove to maintain but at the cost of a reckless liberal-

ity from which his household had to suffer both in deed and in spirit. (101-102)

Attention should be drawn to the correspondence between Mr. Dedalus and the stereotypical characters of *Dubliners* with their lapses into fantasy. Mr. Dedalus consciously creates a false perception of his self-image. This misrepresentation of reality that Mr. Dedalus performs for himself serves to link him with Farrington and Mr. Duffy, who had gone to great efforts respectively to create a mental image of themselves which makes their lives incongruent with reality. But furthermore, this idea of fantasy as destructive of positive self-development is better elucidated here in that this dementia causes Mr. Dedalus's family to suffers over the course of a childhood and an entire novel, rather than the results of previous short stories that largely took place over a small amounts of time and pages.

To understand the importance of liberation from nationalism and foreign oppression it may be useful to examine how Stephen can be a metaphor for the Irish nation, specifically with regards to power structures and language. If Stephen may be accepted as a metaphor, it is then interesting to look at how he tries to shed his own past and his nation's history to break the mould of the existing Irish consciousness and create another definition. With a new definition of Irishness, Stephen may then perhaps create a new future for himself and metaphorically the nation.

Bildungsroman of a nation

Foster speculates that "the elision of the personal and the national, the way history becomes a kind of scaled-up biography, and biography becomes a microcosmic history, is a particularly Irish phenomenon" (xi). The accuracy of this statement is difficult to measure. However, it is not unusual for *Portrait* to be read as both Joyce's biography and as the *Bildungsroman* of Ireland, as the story essentially tells the process of development be it personal or national. The evolution of self or nation in the positive sense is about developing a more sophisticated identity, with a stronger understanding of self and while Foster may chide this reading that seems all too "Irish", it may still prove fruitful in interpreting the character and nation.

The great benefit of a stronger sense of self is having the control to develop independently, leading to autonomy from the restrictive forces that would otherwise create attenuated identities. For these novels, the story of acquiring selfhood applies both on the personal and national level because Stephen's development from childhood to adulthood is connected with developmental ideas of national importance, namely, language and authority. Both language and authority correspond directly to the nation's need to acquire an independent voice apart from that which has been taught by tradition and to create its own authority, rather than be subjected to foreign oppressors.

Stephen is attempting a solution to the problems that were merely illustrated in *Dubliners*, which, of course is more difficult. Stephen, sometime shortly after the preacher's sermon, awakes from a nightmare and after saying his prayers in fear, it should be noted that "he wept for the innocence he had lost" (*Portrait* 150). This one instance may be read as an encapsulation of the maturity of Stephen even at this early point in this novel. Although Stephen is frightened into conformity for the time being, he possesses some self-realisation of responsibility to himself. This quotation reflects the difficulty of honesty in considering one's identity, something that was rare for the characters of *Dubliners*. Because Stephen is self-conscious enough to see the danger of losing a

3 Stephen Dedalus and Irish Identity 71

critical perspective on himself, and even though he temporarily regrets having to be forced to this realisation that he controls his own fate, that his sins are his own fault, he is ultimately rewarded by embracing this understanding that gives him the rationalization to change. However, a slightly more mature Stephen will once again find the strength to change when he realises that by controlling his own fate he need not necessarily give himself to a system that seeks his subservience rather than his development.

That critical self-consciousness is what ultimately keeps Stephen from submitting to nationalism and oppression by reminding him that he is an individual who does not need to be defined by outside forces and institutions. Furthermore, Stephen becomes aware of the power of language to define identity, to be used for oppression and also to be used for liberation.

Stephen, the nation and authority

The forces that compete for the right to construct Stephen's identity are formal apparatuses of authority, namely: the Roman Catholic Church, the British colonial establishment, and the more informal homegrown nationalist movement. In fact, it is Stephen who theorises why the foreign apparatuses have such a powerful role in Ireland:

> The idea that the power of an empire is weakest at its borders requires some modification for everyone knows that the Pope cannot govern Italy as he governs Ireland nor is the Tsar as terrible an engine to the tradesmen of S. Petersburg as he is to the little Russian of the Steppes. In fact in many cases the government of an empire is strongest at its borders and it is invariably strongest there in the

case when its power at the centre is on the wane. (*Stephen* 133)

In this extended passage the reader will notice how the novel has taken advantage of hindsight by giving Stephen these prophetic words that can be understood to anticipate the war of Irish independence from Great Britain. Of course, the comments refer specifically to the Church, which particularly in *Stephen Hero*, is seen as the greater tyrant of the Irish people, as Stephen states:

> The Roman, not the Sassenach, was for him the tyrant of the islanders: and so deeply had the tyranny eaten into all souls that the intelligence, first overborne so arrogantly, was now eager to prove that arrogance its friend. (*Stephen* 52)

However, either interpretation links Ireland with the problem of foreign authorities oppressing the nation. These forces of oppression seek to implement themselves on Stephen through the following avenues: education, conscription and by the location of Ireland's position as peripheral to the world.

Stephen's position in the world is of course Ireland. But more specifically, in one example of Stephen's many lists of order, he puts himself into the widest scope possible, "Stephen Dedalus / Class of Elements / Clongowes Wood College / Sallins / County Kildare / Ireland / Europe / the World / The Universe" (*Portrait* 12). At this young age, perhaps before education and culture could wholly submerge him into the confines of the single perspective that he must struggle against, he is able to think of his identity as linked with the widest scope of humanity and beyond. This outward movement seemingly gives Stephen access to all that is included. It should be noted that the link between Ireland and

Europe is significant for reducing the isolationist nationalism that defines Ireland as separate from the world and also for omitting Ireland as a part of Great Britain. Shortly after this list Stephen wonders, "What was after the universe? Nothing" (*Portrait* 13), which indicates that, at this point, Stephen is not thinking of religion as existing in the same space as his perceptual world. However, no sooner has Stephen recorded these grand ideas than the reader is made aware of the conformity around him as a fellow student; Fleming, composes a poem, "Stephen Dedalus is my name / Ireland is my nation. / Clongowes is my dwelling place / And heaven my expectation" (*Portrait* 13). Fleming's poem may be in jest, but it serves to counteract all of the universal and outward ideas, as in Fleming's version, Ireland is expressly made the only place that Stephen can be a part of, and heaven is the only possible outside context. There is no possibility of movement here as there was in Stephen's version, all is predestined from birth and is intended to define Stephen.

Stephen will eternalise this feeling of peripheral position in the discouragement he feels upon trying to fit himself into a debate with Horace. Realising that he can have no impact on Roman history, but only be a passive reader like so many others who had borrowed the same copy from the library, hurts Stephen:

> It wounded him to think that he would never be but a shy guest at the feast of the world's culture and that the monkish learning, in terms of which he was striving to forge out an esthetic philosophy, was held no higher by the age he lived in that the subtle and curious jargons of heraldry and falconry. (*Portrait* 194)

The issue here is that Stephen is trying to identify with Roman culture and history rather than Irish culture. Because of this peripheral location, Stephen does not yet see the use of studying his own history or trying to write his theory into his own culture. Stephen's fear that he will not be able to figure in international debate does not however differ from Doyle's similar situation in "After the Race." Doyle loses the card game in the company of his more established competitors and then fails to see that he cannot play their game at their level. However, while Doyle is unaware of the impossibility of becoming an equal with his English and French competitors, Stephen does realise that he cannot be on level terms with the Romans.

One example of Stephen's ability for realisation comes when describing his fellow student Lynch. Stephen notes that Cranly had nicknamed Lynch "Nero" because he often discussed women. However, "It was possible to accuse his mouth of a Neronic tendency but he destroyed the illusion of imperialism by wearing his cap very far back from a shock forehead" (*Stephen* 124). The juxtaposition of Irish postcolonial culture with that of imperial Rome underscores the anomaly between the two. Even if Stephen is merely joking about this particular Irishman, the metaphor develops similarly as it did in "After the Race." Expressly, the character would have more success in trying to be original than to copy the style of the continentals or in the case of Lynch, the Roman emperor.

Continuing the Irish-Roman comparison, Stephen links the oppression of Roman Catholic religion with Roman imperialism:

> These wanderings filled him with deep-seated anger and whenever he encountered a burly black-vested priest taking a stroll of pleasant inspection through these warrens full of swarming and cringing believers he cursed the farce of Irish Catholicism: an island [whereof] the inhabi-

tants of which entrust their wills and minds to others that they may ensure for themselves a life of spiritual paralysis, an island in which all the power and riches are in the keeping of those whose kingdom is not of this world, an island in which Caesar confesses Christ and Christ confesses Caesar that together they may wax fat upon a starving rabblement which is bidden ironically to take to itself this consolation in hardship 'The Kingdom of god is within you' (*Stephen* 132)

Again, Stephen draws attention to the oppression heaped upon the Irish by the Church and associates the Church's control of the country with that of imperial rule. This passage also makes reference to the collusion of the imperial and the religious authority.

Stephen's allusions to the power of the Roman Church and Empire aside, the novel also provides evidence of the sway that the Church and British Empire held over Stephen's developing Irish generation, in the form of conscription. Stephen listens as a drunken Donovan lists the fellow university students, who will devote themselves to the service of the Empire, "Did you hear the results of the exams? he asked. Griffen was plucked. Halpin and O'Flynn are through on the home civil. Moonan got fifth place in the Indian. O'Shaughnessy got fourteenth" (*Portrait* 228). Bleakly, this is the career of choice for many of the students, and the career that Stephen's father had urged him to apply for. Yet for Stephen, the contradiction of opposing British rule and yet taking a position in their government is one problem; the other is the miserable life that Stephen knows that would await him as a civil servant (*Stephen* 194-195).

Troublingly, Stephen witnesses the power of conscription as it affects the men that would seemingly stand as the most stubborn opposition, namely Madden and his fellow nationalistic followers. Stephen questions the uprising that would prepare with hurling matches rather than participate in the military training offered by the British, which they refuse on nationalistic terms. However, many of these students are studying towards the law and civil service, professions that uphold the same system as the British military. This contradiction inspires Stephen to remark to Madden, "I do not quite follow the distinction you make between administering English law and administering English bullets: there is the same oath of allegiance for both professions" (*Stephen* 61). Stephen's statement leaves little space for any answer besides the condition that law is different from the more brutish physical and military presence of the army. However, Stephen mocks this distinction by pointing to the pettiness of espousing Irish tradition and independence, and parading a party line of non-service to the British, while simultaneously looking to secure a good job in the British government's system of oppression. Stephen again questions his friend:

> And, tell me, how many of your Gaelic Leaguers are studying for the Second Division and looking for advancement in the Civil Service? – That's different, they are only civil servants: they're not ... – Civil be damned! They are pledged to the Government, and paid by the Government. (*Stephen* 61)

Idealistic as Stephen may be, he has thus deconstructed the integrity of a nationalist movement unable to uniformly disassociate itself from the authoritarian power it is meant to dispose of. Stephen's conclusion further links Irish nationalism with British oppression as forces that want to control the national consciousness rather than positively develop independence. However, while the British may have overt, base reasons for their colonisation, Irish nationalism, represented here in the form of the Madden character, only wants what the British have without being able to explain why, namely money and power. The point that Stephen makes is that the nationalist tradition is only a means of displacing the foreign colonial authority and is not a system capable of replacing the void left by supplanting the British system. Nevertheless, nationalism as a system for the displacement of British colonialism may not be suitable either because nationalism may merely merge with colonialism to create a system of oppression that is nationalistic in appearance and rhetoric but, in truth, operating as British colonialism had previously. Gibbons observes that this corruption of nationalism is not an unusual aspect of colonialism, as it "[i]s a two-way (albeit unequal) transaction, and [. . .] many of the concepts requisitioned by nationalist propagandists in defence of Irish culture are, in fact, an extension of colonialism, rather than a repudiation of it" (*Transformations* 156).

This failure of nationalism to dissociate its strategies and goals from the influence of the colonial system it seeks to displace is compounded by the subconscious respect that colonialism has won from the colonised. Colonialism in this sense has made its existence seem so natural that the nation is pressed to decipher what constitutes national philosophy from the examples taught by the coloniser.

The final point of this section concerns the role of education in enforcing colonial oppression. Cairns and Richards note, "By the closing decades of the nineteenth century the catholic Church and Catholicism…were central, as the partners and guarantors of familism and the educator of the people-nation" (63). By controlling the education system and promoting their version of morality, the Church had an enormous power to construct Irish identity. The idea of colonising subjects through education is a common theme in postcolonial writing; the difference in Joyce is that colonialism is seen as being multifaceted. Stephen often disassociates the colonial British oppressor by making comparisons with the Roman Empire, which in Stephen's thought is actually a three-fold empire in terms of the military and governmental imperialism but also in regard to the religious imperialism. As evidenced throughout his education, Stephen is forced to learn the oppressors' history and incorporate it as his own, maintaining the aforementioned point that the governmental and religious imperialisms can here be read as working in collusion:

> The English lesson began with the hearing of the history. Royal persons, favourites, intriguers, bishops, passed like mute phantoms behind their veil of names. All had died: all had been judged. What did it profit a man to gain the whole world if he lost his soul? At last he had understood: and human life lay around him, a plain of peace whereon ant-like men laboured in brotherhood, their dead sleeping under quiet mounds. (*Portrait* 135)

Although it may seem obvious, it is important to note that all of Stephen's formal education is conducted through the Catholic Church's educational services. While this may have been quite ordinary, it serves to colour all of Stephen's learning and thought. As exampled in the lines above, even the history of England works its way back to the Church, for Stephen here understands that the Church's power is more far-reaching than any worldly empire when the soul is taken into consideration. Still, of significant importance is that Stephen will come to associate the Church's teaching as a colonial oppression along side that of Britain. Stephen makes this relation because the Catholic school teaches English history, but more importantly, he sees the Church as functioning in a similar and yet more successful manner. In fact, the Stephen of *Stephen Hero* is evidently far more concerned with the Church's role in exercising authority than the British, as he states:

> The Roman, and not the Sassenach, was for him the tyrant of the islanders: and so deeply had the tyranny eaten into all souls that the intelligence, first overborne so arrogantly, was now eager to prove that arrogance its friend. The watchcry was Faith and Fatherland, a sacred word in that world of cleverly inflammable enthusiasms.
> (*Stephen* 52)

The first aspect of this passage concerns the blame that Stephen heaps on the Church. Of course throughout both novels, the Church has a persuasive influence over Stephen's world. Stephen comes to feel that the Church incessantly demands his conformity to its norms. The Church is able to do this through the education system that rewards conservative Catholic thinking and shuns liberalism, through a society that rejects the outsider and finally, through Stephen's family, which further pressures him to conform. Yet despite this opposition, Stephen is able to separate himself from his place and position as he considers the danger of resigning himself to this institution. Furthermore, Stephen also aligns British influence on Irishness with the Church's influence, in that both seek to constrict the idea of Irishness to a base level of definition, rather than allow any room for the possibility of expansion.

Crucially, Stephen does find the Church institutions as oppressive and he directly links the Church's goal with that of imperialism. Although Stephen does not explain how, he does nevertheless suggests that the Church benefits from imperialism in an:

> Island in which Caesar [professes] confesses Christ and Christ confesses Caesar that together they may wax fat upon a starveling rabblement which is bidden ironically to take to itself this consolation in hardship "the Kingdom of God is within you." (*Stephen* 132)

A part of this passage was previously examined, but in the continuation here the reader may conclude from Stephen's ideas that the Church exchanges the opportunity under colonial rule to exercise the maximum amount of authority on Ireland in return for ignoring the damaging effects of an unchecked religious and governmental authority. The uncontrollable power of a religion that defines national identity, and a foreign government that is able to find shelter in the ambivalence of this all-powerful societal structure, result in a paralysed nation. The desire to decolonise is checked by the Church that discourages change. In another source consider Joyce's parallel poetic reflection of Ireland's entrapped political and ideological identity as "Where Christ and Caesar are hand and glove" (*Gas* 243). This difficulty may be most visible in the nationalist movement that so actively seeks to align itself with the traditional idea of Irishness, of course this idea of Irishness has been sculpted as including the Church to the point that Irishness is "Catholicity" as well. Therefore the nationalists' desire to deconstruct the foreign governmental oppressor is subverted by the Church's ambiguity about attacking the governmental system that has allowed the Catholic religious structures and ideology to prosper.

The Church, the British colonial establishment, and Irish nationalism are all competing, and at times collaborating, in the use of authority, or more specifically, the right to define the national notion of Irishness. Reading Stephen as an allegory for this situation provides the reader with the problems of deconstructing these constrictive structures so that an independent identity and sovereignty can be forged. However, these physical and ideological structures are not the only level of authority with which Stephen must contend to create himself independently. He must first find his voice and of course his language.

Stephen, the nation and language

In broad terms, a fundamental theme of the novel is Stephen's mastery of language, from the first page where he passively listens to his father's story of the moocow, to writing the journal that constructs Stephen as the narrator of his own story. The apparent postcolonial implication is in the development of Stephen's written account of his city and nation. On a personal level, Stephen feels he has an understanding of his culture and he has the self-confidence to believe that his perspective is worth exploring. On a national, allegorical level, Stephen figures as the "Irish" taking control of their own image and identity through writing, thus granting language a great deal of power.

From a young age, Stephen is aware of the terrific power of language. For example, at Christmas dinner when he wonders, "What was the name the woman had called Kitty O'Shea that Mr Casey would not repeat?" (*Portrait* 36), Stephen is initially mildly interested in the power of this word, but as he matures, his mind's attention is increasingly engrossed with the power of words, as exemplified by the occasion where he reads the word "foetus" carved into a school desk:

> The sudden legend startled his blood: he seemed to feel the absent students of the college about him and to shrink from their company. A vision of their life, which his father's words had been powerless to evoke, sprang up before him out of the word cut in the desk. A broad-shouldered student with a moustache was cutting in the letters with a jack-knife, seriously. Other students stood or sat near him laughing at his handiwork. One jogged his elbow. The big student turned on him, frowning. He was dressed in loose grey clothes and had tan boots. (*Portrait* 102-103)

Stephen's imagination is language-based, all of this imagery is triggered by one word that is charged with associations. Furthermore, this passage demonstrates the power of this word to set off Stephen's imagination in his fantasy of these make-believe students. This timid picture of Stephen may be related to the problems that he initially has with language's connection to nationality, as Stephen is subservient to the English language spoken by those of the English nationality.

When language becomes linked with nationality and identity, as is the case in the notorious funnel/tundish debate between Stephen and the Dean of Studies, Stephen loses his confidence. In addition, it is in terms of the question of the authority of language that Stephen is at first degraded, and later liberated, simply by a word-definition that symbolises the authority that English nationality holds over the English language. When the Dean remarks, "Is that called a tundish in Ireland? [. . .] I never heard the word in my life," Stephen is immediately defensive as he defers to the nationality of the speaker, "a countryman of Ben Jonson," rather than consider the possible inaccuracy of the Dean. However, the Dean

3 Stephen Dedalus and Irish Identity

is respectfully addressed, "It is called a tundish in Lower Drumcondra, said Stephen, laughing, where they speak the best English" (*Portrait* 204-205). Of course although the Dean is mistaken, Stephen initially takes this observation with humble subservience. Ironically, Stephen's nervous joking is far more accurate that he can, at the moment, imagine. Stephen's vocabulary exceeds that of the Dean, and this idea correlates with Stephen's previously explored notion that an Empire is stronger at the borders. Stephen has wholeheartedly embraced the English language as his own, evidenced by his reluctance to learn Irish[10] and yet in this conversation with the Dean, a feeling arises of resignation towards the "native" English speaker. This combination leaves Stephen without a first language and the ensuing traumatisation is illustrated by the following interior monologue:

> The language in which we are speaking is his before it is mine. How different are the words home, Christ, ale, master, on his lips and on mine! I cannot speak or write these words without unrest of spirit. His language, so familiar and so foreign, will always be for me an acquired speech. I have not made or accepted its words. My voice holds them at bay. My soul frets in the shadow of his language.
> (*Portrait* 204)

In the most extreme language Stephen is capable of mustering, he expresses the hopelessness of the situation. By putting himself in the place of colonised other, Stephen submits any power over

---

[10] He makes this clear in argument with Davin, "My ancestors threw off their language and took another, Stephen said. They allowed a handful of foreigners to subject them. Do you fancy I am going to pay in my own life and person debts they made? What for?"(*Portrait* 222)

the English language that he should rightfully be able to claim as a native speaker.

This idea is not only evident in the hyper-self-conscious Stephen, but in his fellow students as well. Consider the amount of foreign language and Latin which Stephen and his fellow students use to converse. Perhaps one passage of particular note is Cranly's inane comment, "Feuc an eis super stradam…in Liverpoolio." (*Stephen* 100) This statement in broken Irish, German and Latin, perhaps on one level demonstrates the character's desire to brag of his education, but it also serves to show a group that is not sure what language to speak.

The language-less Stephen is left in the position of always answering to the English nationality for their definition of the language. As English is Stephen's only mode of expression, he is therefore subservient to the English by way of their language and nationality. Mercifully, Stephen realises the inaccuracy of this logic when he discovers the misidentification of the 'local Irish word,' as detailed by his journal entry much later in the novel:

> April 13. That tundish has been on my mind for a long time. I looked it up and find it English and good old blunt English too. Damn the dean of studies and his funnel! What did he come here for to teach us his own language or to learn it from us. Damn him one way or the other!
>
> (*Portrait* 274)

The anxiety that this problem has caused Stephen is remarkable. If the reader is to assume that over the time that elapsed from the meeting with the Dean to this journal entry was a period of sustained fretting for Stephen's soul, then the damage this language authority has inflicted on Stephen, and metaphorically the nation, is momentous. However, as powerful as the authority of language may be, the power of Stephen's epiphany is evenly balanced. In literally articulating the problem and then freeing himself from the power structure, Stephen has liberated himself from the confines of England's English language. In terms of the national metaphor, at this moment he forgives the past, accepting the language as once foreign but now indigenous and allowing for the nation to be able to express itself in its native English voice without the shame of subservience.

There is also the more sweeping matter of language as a means of expression, which provides access to forms of power, legitimacy and escape encompassing, but also expanding beyond, the colonial relationship. For instance, the seabird-girl of *Portrait* inspires Stephen's maxim, "to live, to err, to fall, to triumph, to recreate life out of life!" (*Portrait* 184). This motto, while useful for understanding Stephen's most fundamental epiphany concerning the joy of life, is also important in this instance for the very fact of its articulation: language is a source of power, from which Stephen can justify his independent stance and identity. From a position of having nearly converted to the priesthood, renouncing his humanity and accepting the authority and position of another, now, amid the ironic and mocking cries of those on the beach of "Stephaneforos," Stephen creates an independent philosophy, however simple, as he embraces his humanity and independence. Language, for this reading of Stephen, is the independent expression of thought. It provides the opportunity to communicate by relieving the oppression and providing escape to places of greater possibility.

Stephen needs escape from his confines in a manner similar to previous characters, the remarkable difference is, however, that Stephen's outlet is a healthier alternative to his counterparts in *Dubliners*. However, in the early stages, Stephen struggles to express this idea. The fundamental example is when Stephen attempts a poem:

> From force of habit he had written at the top of the first page the initial letters of the jesuit motto: A.M.D.G. On the first line of the page appeared the title of the verses he was trying to write: To E---C---. He knew it was right to begin so for he had seen similar titles in the collected poems of Lord Byron. When he had written this title and drawn an ornamental line underneath he fell into a daydream and began to draw diagrams on the cover of the book. (*Portrait* 73)

This early attempt on Stephen's part may remind readers of Little Chandler who can picture himself as the artist, but who cannot create art. Furthermore, Stephen is only a mimic; the attempt shows a desire for expression but no ability to express. Because of his oppressive religious training, Stephen first is unable to disassociate this artistic venture from his religion, and therefore, before the opportunity to create this poem independently arises, he has already labelled it with the Jesuit insignia. Furthermore, after religious labelling, the poem then submits itself to the English poetic conventions. Thus far, Stephen has yet to write a line of poetry, but has subconsciously filled his page with the two forces most powerfully aligned in their ability to construct Stephen's notion of language and expression: the text has been unable to escape its context. Fittingly, Stephen then locates himself with the previously studied characters, who were unable to realise their desires and displaced reality by a world of daydream.

However, after these initial failures, Stephen does make progress in expressing the thoughts and feelings that he cannot confide to others or even voice in confession. Stephen can express these inner workings in his secret writing and publishing:

> The foul long letters he had written in the joy of guilty confession and carried secretly for days and days only to throw them under cover of night among the grass in the corner of a field or beneath some hingeless door in some niche in the hedges where a girl might come upon them as she walked by and read them secretly. (*Portrait* 126)

Worthy of particular distinction in this passage is that these declarations are in writing. At this early point in the novel, Stephen finds one of the rewards of writing is the relief of expression, which has a more lasting effect than the more publicly accepted benefits like the prize money or the high marks.

Similar to James Duffy's philosophical reading, Stephen is an avid reader of the thought and art from beyond Ireland. Stephen initially only sees the beauty in European writing and sees no such worth in the literature of Ireland, for example in his stroll to university, the images of Ireland around him inspire thoughts of Gerhart Hauptmann, Guido Cavalcanti, Henrik Ibsen, Aristotle, Aquinas and the Elizabethans. These writers/philosophers from across Europe show the vastness of Stephen's knowledge, but as Seamus Deane notes, "part of the meaning of this programmed journey to the university, with all its attendant associations, is its privacy. Stephen is creating an imaginative world that runs parallel to the actual world he inhabits" (introduction 307). Deane's reading suggests that Stephen has found escape in his European reading by picturing the ideas of these writers despite his location in Ireland. However, the joy of this escape is at this point no different to the release that Duffy may have felt while engaging with European philosophy: in both cases the readers have only one way interaction with Europe. Significantly, Duffy was unable to take the next step of interacting with the philosophy, interpreting it or responding with his own writing and thinking. However, Stephen does develop a response to all of his reading when he begins to interpret his surroundings in his own words rather than continue with quotations. Stephen begins to write the nation and the land as, "crossing Stephen's, that is, my green, remembered that his countrymen and not mine had invented what Cranly the other night called our religion" (*Portrait* 271). Stephen is at once putting Dublin into his own context, or as Deane has noted, 'Stephen is now moving to possess his experience and his Dublin' (introduction 328), meaning that Stephen has granted himself the power to write about Dublin, with a certain legitimacy, previously unimagined. Stephen, in this passage, also further displaces Catholicism's claims, by branding it as a foreign establishment without an inherent right to define the nation.

In conclusion, it is necessary to mention the final moment of the novel where Stephen proclaims his desire "to forge in the smithy of my soul the uncreated conscience of my race" (*Portrait* 290). By writing, Stephen can hope to give a new voice to his nation. However overstated this desire may seem for the still quite young Stephen, it is a major achievement that he has sustained his independence throughout all the trials of his adolescence and it is truly admirable that he has accepted the challenge to develop a new perspective for his nation that for the moment seems to hostilely reject his offerings.

The above passage also expressly identifies Stephen's desires with his nation, which further justifies a reading of Stephen as national symbol or representative of Ireland, rather than as an outsider or individual apart from his surroundings. Given that Stephen wants to create a new voice for this nation, the question is then how can he deal with the old voice, the history and identity of the Ireland that has failed to convert him throughout the novel?

Breaking the pattern of Irish identity and history

Perhaps Stephen's most remarkable characteristic is his stubbornness. While all of those around Stephen are coaxed into conformity, Stephen maintains his independence and his right to create his identity even when he is not sure who he is exactly. Yet despite Stephen's initial confusion, he gradually accepts and embraces that which makes him different, as "[h]e was aware that though he was nominally in amity with the order of society into which he had been born, he would not be able to continue so" (*Stephen* 161). In both novels, and in this passage from *Stephen Hero* specifically, the protagonist understands his position and wills himself to exist in conflict with the "order of society." By doing so Stephen will be at varying degrees of conflict with nearly every character and institution he will encounter. However, this challenge is not one-sided, although Stephen is constantly forced to explain his behaviour, he acts as a catalyst to those around him who must consider his viewpoint.

Stephen essentially finds fault in the binary and isolated view that is so often espoused by his teachers and peers. This limited perspective on the part of Stephen's fellow Dubliners extends to their general representations of history that are too reductive for Stephen, who will desire to develop a more pluralistic approach. It may also be noted that Stephen thus far rejects the importance of history in terms of its relevance in the present. While other characters justify their surroundings or position by history, Stephen finds history to be an obstacle rather than inspiration for independent creation.

Furthermore, Stephen repeatedly rebukes the calls to conform to the institutions that have laid claims to authentic Irishness.

Stephen not only shuns these demands, but also actively deconstructs these institutions' right to control Irish consciousness as he looks to create another, more inclusive, space in which one can also exist and still be Irish.

Detaching history

At first, history is a source of power and justification for Stephen as exampled by his brave journey into the headmaster's office at Clongowes Wood College to report the prefect's unfair punishments. From this scene, Stephen motivates himself with the following idea:

> A thing like that had been done before by somebody in history, by some great person whose head was in the books of history. And the rector would declare that he had been wrongly punished because the senate and the Roman people always declared that the men who did that had been wrongly punished. (*Portrait* 54)

This quote reveals Stephen reacting to what has excluded him: he is thinking inside what is acceptable in relation to the past and to his current social position. The action of young Stephen is essentially giving history the authority, as he attempts to fit into the constructs in which history has been taught to him. In other words, Stephen's understanding of history at this point is limited to a reductive binary vision where, for this example, there are good men and bad men.

However, Stephen will realise that he does not need to consider the past in order to justify his identity; instead he thinks of the inaccuracies that this construction of history creates. For example, Stephen, the once devout Catholic, later will seemingly break free of what he comes to understand as the conformist teachings of the Church by dismissing the authority of the religion. However, Stephen's new position on religion is at times as one-dimensional as was his earlier belief. Stephen refuses to take communion because the symbol represents, "twenty centuries of authority and veneration" (*Portrait* 265). This quote shows Stephen's willingness to separate himself from what the majority may believe as well as ignoring the power of history and authority for the sake of his own ideals and philosophies. In fact Stephen continues that one, "cannot answer for the past" (*Portrait* 265), an idea that further illustrates his eagerness to detach his vision for the future from what is generally prescribed by history as that which is possible. Although Stephen's idealism is commendable to some extent, he has essentially embraced the opposite side of the religious binary, becoming anti-Catholic as opposed to devoutly Catholic. For example, when Stephen's mother asks him to make his Easter duty, it is reported that, "He was much annoyed that his mother should try to wheedle him into conformity by using his sister's health as an argument" (*Stephen* 120). The coldness of this narration, and of Stephen's conviction, makes his philosophy as fanatical as what he wishes to escape.

Although it is understandable that Stephen would like to make a clean break from the entire history and connection of oppression that he associates with the Church or Irish Catholicism, he is doing so at the cost of the well being of those who care for him. Stephen is far more open minded, about religion in particular, when he is asked about believing in the Eucharist, to which he replies, "I neither believe in it nor disbelieve" (*Portrait* 260). This pluralistic idea embodies a far more developed response to the authority that Stephen is trying to combat. Rather than taking the reactionary position, Stephen detaches himself thereby enabling him to see at once the mystery of the sacrament that has played such a role in his upbringing and conversely, the dangers of conforming to what he understands as a foreign body, which is literally proselytising his countrymen.

During the sermon that puts so much fear into Stephen, the Preacher announces that in hell there is no family or country (*Portrait* 131). Although this initially disturbs young Stephen, the idea becomes rather attractive as his opinions mature. Perhaps more than elsewhere, Stephen realises the absurdity of the notions of "Irish" family and country that were alluded to by the Preacher and to which nationalists cling, a point illustrated in the comment of Stephen's fellow student Hughes:

> He declared in ringing Northern accents that the moral welfare of the Irish people was menaced by such theories. They wanted no foreign filth. Mr Dedalus might read what authors he liked, of course, but the Irish people had their own glorious literature where they could always find fresh ideals to spur them on to new patriotic endeavours. Mr. Dedalus was himself a renegade from the Nationalist ranks: he professed cosmopolitism. But a man that was of all countries was of no country – you must have a nation before you have art. (*Stephen* 95)

What this quotation illustrates is the alignment of nationalism and religion with "real" Irishness. For Hughes, art is merely a tool by which the nation's political and ideological goals can be met. Furthermore, this idea reduces the need for outside influence, suggesting that Ireland is actually corrupted by the cosmopolitonism that Stephen espouses. This binary line of thinking mirrors the previously explored religious questions that Stephen encounters. For the nationalists, Irishness can only exist in the accepted forms of nationalism. In a manner similar to his understanding of religion, Stephen must find the right response to nationalism's challenge. In the most positive instances Stephen's responce is again not reactionary, but rather is open to understanding both perspectives from a distance. For example, Stephen thinks of his fellow Jesuit trained students as being very Catholic, patriotic and at times notes that:

> Without displaying an English desire for an aristocracy of substance they held violent measures to be unseemly and in their relations among themselves and towards their superiors they displayed a nervous and (whenever there was question of authority) a very English liberalism. (*Stephen* 155).

Stephen's reflection brilliantly engages the Irish-English binary and, while admitting to the Catholicism and patriotism of his fellow students, he also realises that these seemingly total opposites are linked with some observable similarities as well. By allowing himself a position between the two political ends of Hughes' nationalism and an anti-nationalist position, Stephen affords himself the best perspective from which to judge the situation and decide for himself the best alternative for his independence.

The final instance worth mentioning in terms of understanding Stephen's shift from a binary reaction position to a brand of pluralism is to be found in his dealings with his family. Although, Stephen has reserved some of his most bitter scorn for his parents throughout the novels, he admits to Maurice: "Yet, there are plenty of people who would consider them my best friends for having advised me as they have done. It seems absurd to call them enemies or to denounce them. They want me to secure what they consider happiness" (*Stephen* 204).

Although this familial recognition may be less obviously a national-allegory than Stephen's shift in thinking in connection with religion and nationalism, it does, nonetheless, demonstrate the more pluralistic position that Stephen takes throughout the novel. However, it is still possible to read Stephen's ability to understand his parents' perspective in terms of general history. In other words, Stephen has realised that although the past may be in conflict with his ideal for the future, he can still try to understand why the institutions that use history to justify their aims have attempted to construct Irish identity for themselves.

Perhaps to better understand Stephen's pluralistic position on Irish history, while simultaneously denying its relevance for his future, it is useful to look at more examples. For instance, at one point in Stephen's conversation with the Dean of Studies, Stephen wonders, "from what had he set out" (*Portrait* 204). Stephen here is wondering why an English Protestant switches from the national and religious binary opposites to embrace Irish Catholicism. It is in this moment that Stephen seems to realise that there is something attractive and desirable about his own local context just as he has fantasised and imagined interactions with the lands and cultures of his favourite writers. The realisation that others may actually imagine and fantasise about or embrace Irishness, as the Dean does, shocks Stephen. Whereas Stephen had previously been unable to see any benefit to his nationality, the moment with the Dean, may to some extent, awaken Stephen to the positive sides of his nationality.

That said, Stephen of course does not go so far as to embrace Irish history as glorious or conform to nationalism and religion. In one brilliant comic phrase from Stephen's notebook, he likens the past to statues of women which, "should always be fully draped, one hand of the woman feeling regretfully her own hinder parts"

(*Portrait* 273), meaning that the history of nationalism, religion, the revival will continue to embrace reductive and conservative visions of the nation's past and will indicate how it can not return to past glory. Stephen, while at times sympathetic to the possibility of an alternative version of Irish history, maintains his conviction that embracing past glory, while currently suffering, is useless if the nation's goal is to move on. Due to sacrifice of the reductive history of a productive Irish Ireland, Stephen realises he must break from the ties of the past, "My art will proceed from a free and noble source. It is too troublesome for me to adopt the manners of these slaves. I refuse to be terrorized into stupidity" (*Stephen* 166). In harsh terms Stephen disassociates himself from those who wish to reconstruct their visions of Ireland's past. Furthermore, Stephen will seek to flee from the "stupidity" that stereotypically makes up the Irish character, perhaps most specifically as articulated above nationalism, religion and tradition.

Indeed, Stephen will always look upon authentic Irishness with scepticism. The instance that might best illustrate this point is when Stephen is out in the country and he comes into contact with an Irish peasant. Of course from the Literary Revival, the peasant has often been made to represent authentic Ireland, but rather than admiration or interest in this trope, we see a picture of Stephen who, "sat alone in the car thinking of the beggar's face. He had never before seen such evil expressed in a face" (*Stephen* 214). This instance first illustrates Stephen's sceptical mentality which separates him from the majority. It is with this cold eye, that Stephen has developed, that he is able to form the essential, independent perspective for creating his own understanding.

Yet, the evil that Stephen identifies in the beggar's face goes beyond scepticism and into a more sinister detestation of the face that represents the culture from which he is trying to escape. This final point does not conform to the pluralistic vision of which Stephen at times seems capable. Although Stephen is not able to consistently embrace a pluralistic perspective in these novels, this topic is worth revisiting when we reencounter an older Stephen and friend in *Ulysses*. Presently, however, the question becomes, if Stephen is able to separate himself from Irish history, how will he therefore interpret his nationality that has been defined by those powerful Irish institutions of Church and country, and their respective histories, to create an Irishness of his own?

Deconstructing Irishness

Stephen is repeatedly called on to conform to the institutions of the Church, nationalism and tradition, yet in each case he chooses to extrapolate from these ideologies definitions of Irishness in order to give greater flexibility for his independent creation. However, Stephen's fellow characters often cite his disregard for these institutions as a fault in his Irishness. For example, after joking with the nationalist Davin about his "hurleystick" revolution and the history of the Irish informer, Davin retorts, "I can't understand you....Are you Irish at all" (*Portrait* 219)? Davin has made politics a question of nationality, with which of course Stephen disagrees. Davin furthermore proves his *naïveté* as he recoils from Stephen's unspecified personal story. Therefore, Stephen has figured out what he believes is based on his own judgement rather than on the hereditary reasoning upon which Davin relies. In a similar strain, Stephen's mother links genealogy with Catholicism as she fails to understand Stephen's disloyalty to the Church, "None of your people, neither your father's nor mine, have a drop of anything but Catholic blood in their veins" (*Stephen* 122). Both Davin and Mrs. Dedalus' ideas of Irishness are rooted in the unchangeable sphere of nationality and heritage. Therefore, Stephen's freethinking seems absurd to all parties.

In answer to these reductive notions of Irishness, Stephen perhaps best articulates his stance when in conversation with Cranly:

> I will not serve that which I no longer believe whether it call itself my home, my fatherland or my church: and I will try to express myself in some mode of life or art as freely as I can and as wholly as I can, using for my defence the only arms I allow myself to use-silence, exile, and cunning. (*Portrait* 268-269)

This passage shows Stephen's willingness to abandon the institutions that have tried to force him to conform, but by exiling himself, by listening and then bringing his own interpretation to his nationality, Stephen hopes to enlighten those who did not question their identity. What goes unsaid in Stephen's idea is any notion of overthrowing the existing institutions or identity; instead he chooses the more passive creation of an alternative.

Possibly the passage more relevant in this regard comes from Stephen's conversation with Davin, as Stephen attempts to explain his resistance to the nationalist cause: "When the soul of a man is born in this country there are nets flung at it to hold it back from flight. You talk to me of nationality, language, religion. I shall try to fly by those nets" (*Portrait* 220).

Stephen is essentially labelling the traditions and institutions that dictate Irishness as a hindrance; he speculates that by avoiding these nets, the Irish person might be able to live independently, rather than be 'caught' and defined. Thus far, this chapter has tried to show how Stephen has been in conflict with the ideologies of nationality and religion, as well as showing how

Stephen has concerned himself with language as a primary tool of oppression and liberation.

But perhaps this passage should also be read as an instance of in terms of Joyce's brilliant use of double-entendre: when Stephen states that he will fly "by" these nets, it most obviously occurs to the reader that he will avoid these institutions that he harps on throughout the novels. However, considering the amount of consideration that nationality, language and religion receive in both novels, as well as in *Ulysses*, perhaps, Stephen will fly "by" as in "with the aid of" these significant words. If this alternative meaning is accepted, then Stephen once again proves his willingness to think bilaterally. By using the institutions of conformity to articulate his ideology, given that they are unavoidably connected to his nation's consciousness, he creates an ideology independent of, and yet with the aid of, the past.

To conclude this idea, let us take into account Stephen's journal entry from April 14th, where he recounts the story of John Alphonsus Mulrennan, who while visiting the west of Ireland, met an old man who spoke Irish and had a rather simple understanding of the world. Stephen initially feels hatred against this man who like the peasant with the evil face in the country represents "authentic Ireland": "I fear him. I fear his redrimmed horny eyes. It is with him I must struggle all through this night till day come, till he or I lie dead, gripping him by the sinewy throat till…Till what?" (*Portrait* 274).

Had Stephen's musing ended here, he would have reduced himself to reactionary thinking, by taking up the opposite position to traditional or authentic Irishness. Yet as the quote mentions, this sort of struggle would leave either Stephen defeated for the revival to continue, or the old man defeated by a new vision of Ireland completely disconnected from its past. Intriguingly, Stephen continues his thought, "Till he yield to me? No. I mean him no harm" (*Portrait* 274). Stephen has realised that he does not need to destroy the past to envision the future. Stephen's goal to forge 'the uncreated conscience' of his race, may be just that, uncreated, but able to exist in parallel, with the existing conscience of his race.

As Stephen prepares to leave Ireland, and begin his writing career, it would seem that he has freed himself from nationalism, religion and language, and is now in a position to create a new Irish nationality. However, what has gone unnoticed in Stephen's assessments of the nation, and in this assessment of Stephen's philosophy, are the shortcomings of Stephen's thinking. Take briefly for instance, Stephen's notions of class from this passage while on the train:

> The carriage smelt strongly of peasants (an odour the debasing humanity of which Stephen remembered to have perceived in the little chapel of Clongowes on the morning of his first communion) and indeed so pungently that the youth could not decide whether he found the odour of sweat [unpleasant] offensive because the peasant sweat is monstrous or because it did not now proceed from his own body. He was not ashamed to admit to himself that he found it [unpleasant] offensive for both of these reasons. (*Stephen* 209)

Stephen here, as he has done elsewhere in both novels, considers his superiority of class in relation to Irish peasants. Perhaps Stephen's attitude is based on his intellectual superiority to the peasants, who for nationalists embodied the essential literary function of showing forth an image of the Irish in which avoidance of the English vices was achieved through acceptance of the rigid moral guidelines of Irish Catholicism (Cairns and Richards 71). However even if this is the case, Stephen fails to disassociate literature from reality, as this sort of class distinction could hardly be welcomed in a new Irishness, as there is a medium way to be chosen between the Abbey theatre's idyllic and mythological vision of Irish peasantry and Stephen, who realises that the future of Irish identity can not be by way of a return to this backwardness that was always alien to him.

From his treatment of his mother, his dying sister, whores, and Emma, it can often be noted that Stephen's way with words does not apply to his conversations with women. In fact, it often seems that Stephen has no understanding of women. Gibbons has made the observation of Irish poetry that, "female figures are endowed with allegorical status at the expense of the interests of living women in the real world" (*Transformations* 20). However this analysis seems to accurately apply to Stephen's literary interpretation of the world around him, as if women are to be read. At one point Stephen thinks of Emma, "Yes, I liked her today. A little or much? Don't know. I liked her and it seems a new feeling to me" (*Portrait* 275). Stephen's interpretation of Emma here is at once totally self-referential and concerned with his interpretation of her, rather than his interaction with her. Also consider Stephen's wild plea to Emma: " That's all...Then I thought I would run after you and say that to you...Just to live one night together, Emma, and then to say goodbye in the morning and never to see each other again!" (*Stephen* 177). Stephen, by ignoring her position, opinion, religion and character, attempts to force her into a situation that would clearly be against everything that Emma's character would seem to symbolise. Stephen's mistake here is his inability to imagine the other's perspective, as he selfishly seeks his own ends.

Stephen's accomplishment is his articulation of the problems that were suffered in *Dubliners*, which he does so masterfully. Stephen has also attempted to answer those problems, but despite giving his listeners and readers some clues, he essentially leaves us without a clear answer. So if it is not Stephen who answers the question of a new Irish identity, who will?

Chapter 4
An Alternative Definition of Irish Identity: Stephen, History and Bloom's Inclusive Irishness

"This triviality made him think of collecting many such moments together in a book of epiphanies" (*Stephen* 188). This quotation from *Stephen Hero* seems to predict the format of the ensuing text that this study of Joyce will investigate: *Ulysses*. However, at this point it becomes increasingly important for the reader to distinguish the author's separateness from the characters, as the Stephen of *Ulysses* could not have written a book like *Ulysses* by June 1904. Despite the strides Stephen has taken in the previous novels, which were developed in the preceding chapter, Stephen has regressed by the opening of the "Telemachus" episode. Having failed to write, to gain a reputation, his escape to Europe has been unsuccessful. In fact, the man of act five of *Portrait* has become the boy of chapter one of *Ulysses* as Stephen is now a wholly self-conscious character to be juxtaposed with his former arrogant disposition. In fact, Attridge notes:

> The beginning of *Ulysses* both continues and retroactively transforms the ending of *A Portrait*, exposing Stephen Dedalus's heroic ambitions as an artist at the close of the earlier text to the possible accusation of a self-deceived posturing when we learn in the later text of their unimpressive outcome. (*Cambridge Companion* 25)

Taking into account the shortcomings at the conclusion of the last chapter, it may become more plausible to read the previous Stephen as only the beginning of the articulation of the problem of Irish identity and colonialism, which apparently was unsolved by the conclusion of *A Portrait of the Artist as a Young Man* and *Stephen Hero*.

It should also be noted that the Dublin of *Ulysses* is the same Dublin of the previously studied texts, complete with colonial trappings, constrictive religion and limited nationalist alternatives that fail to provide a positive direction for Irish identity. Stephen is still inwardly struggling with his role and his reaction to those nets that he previously vowed to fly by. Unable to solve the tasks set out in the previous text, Stephen becomes lost and allows deficiencies of his character discussed in the previous chapter to develop further or be eclipsed by the more pressing need for a renewed sense of self. While Stephen continues to search for his lost direction, a possible alternative solution is unexpectedly offered in the unusual character of Leopold Bloom.

Sharing the book with Stephen, the reader may begin to see Bloom's attributes offering a counterpoint to Stephen's failures, as Bloom's philosophy seems to offer a solution to Stephen's struggle for autonomous identity. Not the typical 'Irish' character or hero, Bloom is the "other" or a minority living alongside a largely homogeneous nation in terms of religion, ethnicity and attitude. To these aspects of Irishness, Bloom is foreign, but he is still nationally "Irish" with the justification that, "I was born here. Ireland" (430). In this regard, Bloom represents the otherness that already exists in Ireland. From Bloom's perspective, his otherness also affords an alternative perspective from which to view Ireland's culture. Importantly, Bloom takes an avid interest in Ireland and actively tries to understand the aspects of the culture that are foreign to him, which gives the text an opportunity to objectively criticise the culture and propose a future that could incorporate Bloom and all others into the identity of "Irish".

A solution for Ireland's crisis of identity has been the focus throughout the previous chapters; Bloom's understanding of his identity represents the conclusion of Joyce's longstanding attention to this Irish identity problem as *Finngans Wake* explores identity issues beyond the scope of *Ulysses* and the previously studied text. Bloom essentially allows for a flexibility that makes absolute definition impossible. In contrast to characters that represent static definitions of identity, Bloom's is flexible and ultimately provides the direction that Joyce's writing advises Ireland to embrace as a means of circumventing a binary choice of colonialism or exclusionary nationalism. This simple philosophy of rejecting binary identity groups who have previously tried to claim the right to control Irish identity, places Bloom in a unique role, whereby he can independently judge his surroundings to ultimately demonstrate why a fixed definition of Irish identity should never have been the teleological goal of the Irish.

Essentially, this chapter seeks to expand on Cheng's ideas of imaging nations and imaging the future of the nation, thereby reading *Ulysses* as deconstructing the restrictive options that Ireland faced when given the opportunity to create a national identity. What the allegory that Bloom's character provides is a constructive way of developing a new national consciousness outside of the previous model that could open Irish identity to far more possibilities. For Irish writing, this includes the opportunity to write Ireland without having to be a part of, or representing, the majority culture or to represent a finite idea of Irishness.

Accepting history and the representations of colonial Ireland

From the final pages of "Ithaca", it seems that the narrator is directly addressed as the question arises, "Which event or person emerged as the salient point of his narration?" a question that is answered by, "Stephen Dedalus, professor and author" (868). Whether "his" is referring to the narrator or to Bloom cannot be clear, but either way, the quote supports the importance of continuing to follow Stephen as one of, if not the main, characters of the text. Stephen's day in *Ulysses* might seem largely unremarkable for the reader without knowledge of the prior texts. However, for those familiar with Stephen, the opening of *Ulysses* discovers that the character has failed to advance himself or any of his goals. In fact, Stephen's first words reflect the continuation of one of the problems that halted his growth in the previous texts, namely the colonial presence that still remains, as he asks Mulligan, "How long will Haines stay in this tower" (2). Haines is just one representative of a colonial British presence that is more visible in *Ulysses* than the previous texts. The colonial presence is not only an impediment to Irish political and ideological independence, but also as developed in the previous text and further explored in *Ulysses*, a force which inspires an exclusive brand of nationalism with which Stephen must again contend.

Perhaps more worrying for Stephen is his loss of focus. In *Portrait* Stephen begins a journal to write his nation and proclaim his intentions to create a new Ireland, yet the Stephen of *Ulysses* now seems unsure of his direction or audience. It is important to study the difficulties Stephen encounters in creating an Irish identity which are illustrated here, because the problems that Stephen encounters now are needed to later understand Bloom's counterpoint.

Overt reminders of colonial identity
More so than in the previous texts, *Ulysses* visually reminds the reader that Dublin is a colonial setting. The taciturn salient image is that of city centre Dublin, as the journalistic title has it, "In the

heart of the Hibernian metropolis," only to be followed by the introduction, "Before Nelson's pillar" (147). This quotation continues with a list of trams and their destinations all over Dublin, reminding the reader that Dublin life moves around this symbol of British presence and authority. Nelson's pillar in this instance seems to function unnoticed by the public, as a mute overseer to Dublin. Gibbons remarks:

> Public monuments are expressions of official memory, and bear witness to the power of the state to legitimate its triumphant versions of the past, and assert its authority over its citizens. By their imposing presence, and their control of public space, they stand in stark contrast to the memories of the vanquished which attach themselves to fugitive and endangered cultural forms. (*Transformations* 145)

The monuments and images of colonialism, religion and nationalism all abound in Joyce's Dublin because they create an unspoken reminder of colonisation in the minds of these characters.

Stephen takes notice of the pillar, prompting the story of Anne Kearns and Florence MacCabe. Stephen titles this story "A Pisgah Sight of Palestine or the Parable of the Plums" (189), and it details the outing of two old Dublin women who make a day of taking in the view from atop the pillar while eating plums and admiring the vantage point. One possible reading is that Stephen is merely forwarding a vulgar anecdote, as some of the journalists seem to assume. For one, the pillar makes for an obvious phallic image, with the ensuing gag of "Two old Dublin women on the top of Nelson's pillar" (187). This sexual metaphor is continued when Stephen elaborates that "they are afraid the pillar will fall [. . .]. But it makes them giddy to look so they pull up their skirts." This fairly straightforward sexual imagery and metaphor is met with the response, "Easy all, Myles Crawford said, no poetic licence. We're in the archdiocese here" (187). Crawford's comments at once demonstrate the journalistic fear of censorship as well as the acknowledgment that this is something of an immoral parable. This reading is continued by Stephen's inclusion of the jibe at Nelson's personal reputation as the women, "settle down on their striped petticoats, peering up at the statue of the onehandled adulterer" (187). This reading portrays Nelson as the central debaucher of the city corrupting those around him such as these two vestals. However, Stephen's story could also be interpreted as indicating that the pillar simply offers the best vantage point of the city, and metaphorically that the British are firmly in control in this established position of authority. Kiberd has explained the significance of this as follows: "He signalizes the British 'occupation', as the church steeples just mentioned indicate the Roman 'occupier'" (introduction 999). The collusion of Church and State is a recurring theme throughout *Ulysses* and is well demonstrated in this image of the two defining powers towering and controlling the skyline of Dublin. The underlying value of this interpretation is to understand Joyce's commitment to underlining the colonial presence as a factor in the moribund state of Irish consciousness. The unnoticed presence of the colonial hegemony, becomes like the religion, a given, unchecked in its authority to shape the nation.

In another encounter with the static reminders of empire, Bloom is confronted with images of the conquerors as he enters the brothel section of Dublin. Bloom, with more perception than the previous examples, makes associations with these images:

An Alternative Definition of Irish Identity 109

> From Gillen's hairdresser's window a composite portrait shows him gallant Nelson's image. A concave mirror at the side presents to him lovelorn longlust lugubru Booloohoom. Grave Gladstone sees him level, Bloom for Bloom. He passes, struck by the stare of truculent Wellington but in the covex mirror grin unstruck the Bonham eyes and fatchuck cheekchops of Jollypoldy the rixdix doldy. (566)

This passage contrasts the passive cuckold Bloom, in the hostile environment of Nighttown, surrounded by these threatening images of British subjugators, who serve to judge or intimidate him. Furthermore, it is worth noting that these images abound in the undesirable section of the city, perhaps a jeer against another feature introduced by the colonists alongside the arrival of the "water closet" that is mocked throughout the text.

Besides these static symbols of the empire, there is the real presence of the colonists in the form of the Viceroy. Of the Viceroy's appearance in "Wandering Rocks," Kiberd notes:

> In this episode, the respective paths traced by church (Fr. Conmee) and State (the Viceroy) do not intersect at any point, as if to suggest the tacit truce which has permitted them to carve up Ireland between them: but Joyce is also at pains to emphasize that, unlike the generally deferential Dubliners evoked in these pages, neither Stephen nor Bloom pays homage to the occupying power. (Introduction 1031)

Kiberd's point further establishes the church and state collusion developed as before in the skyline metaphor. The quote also addresses one of the links between Bloom and Stephen, in that neither shows any sense of gratitude to the Viceroy or Father Conmee. By omission, this point concludes that the majority of the characters in this chapter do pay respect to these symbols of authority. In a summary of the cavalcade's journey, the narrator comments, "The viceroy was most cordially greeted on his way through the metropolis" (324). Although this could possibly be intended as irony, based on the reactions of Simon Dedalus and the barmaids Miss Douce and Miss Kennedy, it seems truthful. The lack of an angry reaction to the Viceroy's presence and the actual amount of positive interest makes for a divided sense of national opinion.

Further encounters with the colonial image worth mentioning include the one-legged sailor who cries, "For England [. . .] home and beauty" (289). Depressing in its description of the soldier's debilitation and the economic alliance with England, this quotation is also ironic for the sympathy that the song provokes as a coin is tossed from Molly's window to the soldier while the street urchins aid him; the soldier suffered for England, yet must survive on the mercy of the Irish. This quote is interesting for representing the end of an Irishman's British military career, and also for its ironic contrast with the scene in which Bloom witnesses the attire of young Irishmen on the beach. As the "Nausicaa" chapter opens, Bloom watches, "[. . .] Tommy and Jacky Caffrey, two little curly-headed boys, dressed in sailor suits with caps to match and the name H.M.S." (449-450). Dressing boys in British military clothing was a common fashionable practice[11] and undermines the goals of Irish nationalism, by symbolically giving the children at

---

[11] Kiberd makes this point in his notes, and furthermore attributes it to Arthur Griffith, who criticizes, 'those anglicised parents who dressed their sons in the naval uniforms of His Majesty's Ships' (Kiberd, *Introduction* 1089).

this early age to the ideology of the coloniser. The metaphor continues on the beach as the twins fight over a sandcastle as the narrator notes, "every little Irish-man's house is his castle [. . .]" (451), further identifying these children with the coloniser as the phrase would more customarily read "every Englishman's house." Then consider the correlation of the child who plays as colonist and the man who works as colonist. Bloom and Stephen both perceive the danger that colonialism poses in making the nation conform, specifically targeting the national identity, forcing the internalisation of colonial values that would make an Irishman accept the role of British soldier, lose a leg, and yet still sing a nationalist song for England.

The continued presence of British colonialism is not only marked in the British symbols and persons, but in the ensuing reaction to colonialism in the form of Irish nationalism. Like the previous texts, *Ulysses* will confront the nationalists' role in existing as binary opposite to colonialism which poses a further complication to any independent creation of a free Irish consciousness. Through Stephen's criticism and Bloom's observation of the absurdities of ignorant exponents of nationalism, *Ulysses* will seek to undermine nationalist philosophy.

One example of nationalism perverting Irishness can be read in the character Cissy Caffery, who may figure as the female symbol of Ireland. This reading is particularly conceivable because of the available references with the Yeats play *Cathleen Ni Houlihan*. One critic usefully interprets the play for this parallel:

> Ireland is anthropomorphised into an old woman, who takes a young man, Michael Gillane, from his wedding to fight and die for her. The mythic message is that the chil-

dren of the nation must be willing to give their lives for their nation. (O'Brien 200)

Given the theatrical style of "Circe," Cissy can be read as a reference to the overt nationalism and anthropomorphism that the Yeats play features.

After an initially brief encounter, Stephen becomes entangled with Cissy, and her accompanying soldiers,[12] outside Mrs Cohen's brothel, to whom Stephen addresses his remark, "You are my guests. The uninvited" (686). Stephen's mock welcome to these British soldiers may remind the readers of the Citizen's cry, "We want no more strangers in our house" (420), which was itself another echo of mother Ireland in "Cathleen Ni Houlihan." Private Carr mistakenly perceives Stephen's comment as an insult against Cissy, takes offence and threatens violence. When the Voices protest that Cissy has no reason to be insulted, Cissy defends the Private's actions by stating, "But I'm faithful to the man that's treating me though I'm only a shilling whore" (687). Cissy's boast demonstrates a rare but present British-Irish alliance. Cissy as mother Ireland in this reading proves that nationality is not important while also mocking the virtue of Irish nationalism's picture of Irish femininity.

This reading furthermore joins the image of militant Britain with wanton Ireland as fitting bed partners, a matching critique of both nations' national identities. This reading develops because of a comment that Bloom makes to Cissy as the Private becomes more angered and a fight is about to ensue: Bloom "(Shakes Cissy Caffrey's shoulders) Speak, you! Are you struck dumb? You are

---

[12] Cissy is not the first girl of the collection to get involved with an Englishman, as we note Bloom's daydream of Emmett's hanging and Emmett's bride who marries the Oxford man (401).

An Alternative Definition of Irish Identity   113

the link between nations and generations. Speak, woman, sacred lifegiver" (694). The lines may again link this dramatic sequence with "Cathleen Ni Houlihan," specifically; this impression further develops if Cissy is read as the symbol of Ireland temporarily embracing whoever is willing to fight for her like Yeats' Cathleen. Bloom, realising the outcome of such a confrontation, attempts to make this symbol of the nation denounce the violence she selfishly demands. This interpretation differs from the Yeats play in that the Gillane family tries to reason with Michael as opposed to the old woman who urges him on the fight, but Bloom realises that the source of the problem is, in part, the nationalist representation of Ireland that encourages violence. Bloom's intervention nearly succeeds as Cissy's cries out, "He insulted me but I forgive him" (697). If Irish nationalism could somehow articulate the unnecessary rationale for violence that it creates, than perhaps the binary conflict would not have to extend to such extreme conclusions.

Another critique of Irish nationalism raised throughout *Ulysses* is the presence of a disguised British militarism existing behind the visage of Irish nationalism. To demonstrate the presence of British militarism in Irish nationalism it is firstly useful to look at how nationalists criticise Englishness, as is stereotypically done so by the Citizen:

> Their syphilisation, you mean, says the citizen. To hell with them! The curse of a goodfornothing God light sideways on the bloody thicklugged sons of whores' gets! No music and no art and no literature worthy of the name. Any civilisation they have they stole from us. Tonguetied sons of bastards' ghosts. (421)

The Citizen as chief xenophobe and Anglophobe, reiterates a point often made elsewhere in the text, simply that the British Empire does not deserve the reputation or respect bestowed upon it by Ireland and the world. With typically confused logic, his point that the British create poor art is contradicted when he claims that what is produced by Britain is actually *high* quality Irish art. The Citizen's tirades against England often conflict with his secret admiration of Britain as his speech continues to be one of praise for the British Navy. While becoming swept up in his own nationalist rhetoric the Citizen proclaims his vision of the future of the Irish Navy:

> Our harbours that are empty will be full again, Queenstown, Kinsale, Galway, Blacksod Bay, Ventry in the kingdom of Kerry, Killybegs, the third largest harbour in the wide world with a fleet of masts of the Galway Lynches and the Cavan O'Reillys and the O'Kennedys of Dublin when the earl of Desmond could make a treaty with the emperor Charles the Fifth himself. And will again, says he, when the first Irish battleship is seen breasting the waves with our own flag to the fore, none of your Henry Tudor's harp, no, the oldest flag afloat, the flag of the province of Desmond and Thomond, three crowns on a blue field, the three sons of Milesius. (425)

In this extended passage, the Citizen, without fully realising it, is essentially expressing his vision of the Irish industry and military mimicking the success of the British and then dominating the waves with the same system that was earlier despised when identified with Britain. The Citizen here fits into Fanon's idea of mimicry: "The native is an oppressed person whose permanent dream is to become the persecutor" (41). Perhaps not all natives would have this desire as Fanon suggests, but the vindictive and subconscious desire to have the coloniser's power is understandable and accurate for reading the Citizen. The underlying Britishness of Irish nationalism is later developed again in the singing of the nationalist song "God Save Ireland" which is reimagined with the attributes of Britain: "Beer, beef, business, bibles, bulldogs, battleships, buggery and bishops. Whether on the scaffold high. Beer-beef trample the bibles. When for Irelandear" (556).

This mixture of seemingly unrelated subjects actually exposes the link in common ideologies, as both are merely forms of nationalism. A final note of similarity worth mentioning is the nationalist Citizen's encounter with British Major Tweedy. In this satirical moment from "Circe" the two characters, that would typically be understood as opposite side of the political spectrum, demonstrate their likeness: "Major Tweedy and the Citizen exhibit to each other medals, decorations, trophies of war, wounds. Both salute with fierce hostility" (693). The above exposes Irish nationalism of the sort espoused by the Citizen as being a mirror of the British nationalism that is at times mocked, detested and yet envied.

The colonial presence contributes to the setting of *Ulysses* by consciously or unconsciously locating all of Ireland in a state of oppression. Cheng describes the importance of the British presence as such:

> Imperial history is very much an oppressive nightmare of the present from which it is hard to awake-if for no other reason than that its oppressive presence and hegemonic, discursive terminology is written all over the face of Ireland and of its cultural construction, and thus forms the

hour-by-hour subtext and context of all their thoughts and experiences. (169)

Cheng's reading highlights the subtle importance of the colonial presence for providing an enforced, violent history that powerfully affects the national consciousness and identity, as can be understood through the character's interior and outward interaction with their place. For Stephen, more sensitive to all things intellectual than the previous characters, the history of Ireland's colonial servitude will be most damaging for his fragile psyche.

The consequences of colonial identity for Stephen

One of the first adjustments that the reader will notice in *Ulysses*, is Stephen's newfound self-consciousness. Ian McBride has speculated that "[t]he relationship between memory and identity is always a two-way one, with ideas of the communal past setting limits to the perceptions and aspirations of the current generation" (*History* 13). Although Stephen is the same character as in *Portrait* and *Stephen Hero*, his interest in himself has developed into a self-conscious self-criticism rather than the overtly societal criticism that seemed to focus on all of Ireland but himself in the previous novels. Indeed McBride's comment seems hauntingly true for the Stephen of *Ulysses*, as this Stephen fails to shatter the constraints of the national identity because of the historical curse he seems to envision for his country.

After the gibes of one of Stephen's most serious detractors, Stephen is for the first time in the text made unsure of himself. When Buck criticises Stephen's second hand clothing, Stephen replies, "They fit well enough" (5), this initially cool response contrasts with Stephen's sentiment later expressed in, perhaps, a spirit of self- mocking, "My Latin quarter hat. God, we simply must dress the character" (51). Stephen here admits his newfound self-awareness and this comment seems to demonstrate that his image is more important that his prior response would indicate.

Buck encourages the first instance of Stephen's self-consciousness by attacking Stephen's appearance, "Look at yourself, he said, you dreadful bard", at which point the narrative shifts into Stephen's interior monologue as he looks into a mirror and reflects, "As he and others see me. Who chose this face for me? This dogsbody to rid of vermin" (5). These inward comments begin Stephen's consideration of his image. Stephen's self-consciousness will extend from here beyond his physical appearance, but also to his failures, his history and his future. Buck, sensing Stephen's introspection, cruelly seeks to further exploit what seems a tender subject by taking the mirror away and proclaiming, "The rage of Caliban at not seeing his face in a mirror, he said" (6).

Consider the implication that this comparison of Stephen and Caliban means for national identity by linking Stephen to the colonised other, Caliban. This suggests that Irish identity unrealistically equates Ireland as equal to Britain, or as Cheng has offered, this passage might be a take on "the rage of the Irishman precisely at seeing his face represented in the English mirror as Caliban, and the parallel rage of not seeing in one's reflection oneself as one's own master" (152). Mulligan's comment may be misinformed, yet it insightfully interprets Stephen as presenting an image that is a disjointed self-perception. Although Stephen will deny this assertion, the comment provides a perspective from which to judge some of Stephen's failures. Most notably Stephen's mummery to impress those around him, as Kiberd notes that Stephen "may be theatricalized in the manner of a colonized male who seems able to play every part – Aristotle, Jesus, Lucifer,

Swift, Shakespeare, Hamlet, Kevin Egan – except his own" (introduction 958). This point is most visibly demonstrated by Stephen's behaviour in the presence of the library intellectuals who fail to realise the agony they inflict upon Stephen's ego. Stephen had earlier articulated the problem of selling his artistic genius to England, when he reflects, "For them too history was a tale like any other often heard, their land a pawn-shop" (29-30), meaning that Irish artists who sell their ideas to the English tradition, are in effect adding their national heritage to the plundered riches of Britain.

Yet Stephen among this Anglo-Irish group of exclusive intellectuals contradicts his earlier idealism and becomes desperate to sell his worthiness and intelligence. While Stephen advances his theory of *Hamlet*, he coaches himself to "[w]ork in all you know. Make them accomplices" (241). Stephen here tries to accommodate and assimilate himself, however, as he continues to attempt to control the conversation he finds his audience only partially receptive to his argument. Stephen's confidence quickly begins to decline as he struggles with himself, "What the hell are you driving at? I know. Shut up. Blast you! I have reasons [. . .] Are you condemned to do this" (266)? Stephen, losing his hold of the audience, must begin to sense the irony of his efforts to impress this group.

Stephen's problem is that the audience finds his argument laborious. Stephen's wish to impress is capped as this opinion is offered, "You are a delusion, said roundly John Eglinton to Stephen. You have brought us all this way to show us a French triangle. Do you believe your own theory?" To which, Stephen humbly and yet annoyingly can only reply, "No" (274). By pursuing the ill-fated argument with such force, Stephen has misjudged his audience and done little to gain their respect. Stephen had been previously slighted by this group when the librarian announces, "Mr Russell, rumour has it, is gathering together a sheaf of our younger poets' verses", when no comment is passed by the group to recognise or encourage Stephen's presence and aspirations, Stephen thinks, "See this. Remember" (246). This bitterness is justified, as the library set has never had intentions of including Stephen. Kiberd has noted that by acting for an audience, "[. . .] Stephen is still a colonized subject, endlessly performing roles assigned and applauded by others" (introduction 1014), or in this case not applauded. Stephen reacts emotionally to the emission from Russell's poetry collection, which results in his shameful mummery as he advances a futile theory to an uninterested party.

On two occasions after Stephen's disappointment in the library, he is found referencing his interest in divination. Outside the library Stephen remembers, "Here I watched the birds for augury" (279), and much later an inebriated Stephen wonders, "Where is my augur's rod" (676)? Stephen's self-perception as prophet is unrealistic given his inability to successfully articulate his own ideas, perhaps explaining why a character with such lack of direction has turned to augury. By the conclusion of *Portrait* and *Stephen Hero*, this character seemed poised to actually create a change, as he had seemingly already liberated himself from the imposing majority philosophies and would therefore be in the position to actually create freely. Yet the Stephen of *Ulysses* can only continue to internally promise to forge change. Lost, it seems, is his overt desire to change the national consciousness, instead he changes to the more introspective goal of liberating himself. Stephen marks this point as he motions to his head, "But in here it is I must kill the priest and the king" (688). But even though this intention is brazen, it is also familiar and disappointing.

While self-consciousness may be the most direct explanation for Stephen's failure, the question becomes then, why is Stephen so insecure? The answer is not solely the hurtful words of Buck or the library intellectuals, but Stephen's more developed reservations about the relevance of history to his own identity. Writing of *Dubliners*, but referring indirectly to all of Joyce's work, Cheng explains, "In Joyce's works, the dead, the past, and history inevitably refuse to stay dead—and continue to be "nets" (to use Stephen Dedalus's term) of entrapment one must try to fly by" (103). For instance, Stephen is obsessed with Ireland's position of colonial servitude and this fixation manifests itself as he compares his time as an altar boy to his relationship with Buck, "I am another now and yet the same. A servant too. A server of a servant" (12). Stephen here is defeating himself by assuming this label and role that is only marginally a part of the context of this situation. Stephen continues this line of thinking with the arrival of the milk woman, who to Stephen represents something of the Irish colonial situation. Upon watching the milk woman's interaction with Buck and Haines, Stephen reflects: "A wandering crone, lowly form of an immortal serving her conqueror and her gay betrayer, their common cuckquean, a messenger from the secret morning. To serve or to upbraid, whether he could not tell: but scorned to beg her favour" (15).

This image of Ireland as perpetually subjected to be servant to the foreign master and to be cast in the role of conspiring compatriot is linked with Stephen's confusion as to what alternatives if anything, could circumvent this course. Stephen here seems to fear both of the options, whether servant or betrayer, unable to decide or bring himself to violence. Stephen's artistic future is also attached to this problem, as he explains to Buck, "The problem is to get money. From whom? The milkwoman or from him. It's a toss up, I think," that thought is continued, "I see little hope, Stephen said, from her or from him" (19). Stephen here is afraid of becoming a servant, and fearing he may be unable to gain a reputation in Ireland, he is left in the position of looking to sell himself to Haines, making Stephen a servant in another sense. When Stephen is left alone with Haines a moment later, his thinking continues to focus on the unfavourable position of servitude, as Stephen proclaims, "I am the servant of two masters, Stephen said, an English and an Italian [. . .] And a third, Stephen said, there is who wants me for odd jobs" (24). Stephen again forwards his idea that Irish identity has been enslaved by colonialism, religion and nationalism. What is most remarkable about the difference here is Haines' spin on the situation. Haines, caught unaware, offers a defence by way of deflection, attributing Ireland's problems, even the current situation to history, "We feel in England that we have treated you rather unfairly. It seems history is to blame" (24). Haines' comment initially surprises Stephen, but throughout the remainder of the text it will recur to Stephen with increasing frustration.

In reference to another Irish poet's relationship with history, Deane notes, "It was Mangan's downfall as an artist that he could not free himself from the tragic history of his nation" ("Joyce" 32-33). Indeed this notion of history consuming the Irish future applies to Joyce's hero, as history will become the primary source of Stephen's creative paralysis preventing the articulation of his previous desires. Stephen fears that history has in some way fated his nation and will therefore loom ominously for him as well. The encounter that best illustrates Stephen's anxiety about history's control over his future can be read in his interaction with the schoolmaster, Mr. Deasy. For Stephen, Deasy represents a continuation of the problems presented by Haines, as Deasy attempts to give the apprentice teacher a partial lecture on Irish-British history along with the underlying values of British conservatism. Stephen fails to appreciate the conservative principles or the notion of "English justness", to which he opines, "I fear those big words, Stephen said, which make us so unhappy" (38), associating Deasy's sense of justice with Haines' dismissal of British responsibility. These links strengthen Stephen's phobia about Ireland's history of subjection as his mind wanders into the images of brutality: "Glorious, pious and immortal memory. The lodge of Diamond in Armagh the splendid behung with corpses of papishes. Hoarse, masked and armed, the planters' covenant. The black north and the true blue bible. Croppies lie down" (38).

Stephen's fear presents him with an image of the cruel side of colonial history, which further disturbs his strained vision of national identity. The penultimate articulation is realised in the following quote, "History, Stephen said, is the nightmare from which I am trying to awake" (42). In relation to this famous passage, Gibbons makes the claim that for Stephen, "the past was a destabilizing rather than conservative force" (*Transformations* 169). This apt reading demonstrates the fear that history will never articulate the colonised, who are endlessly doomed to be subservient to the coloniser that holds the proverbial key to the control of history. For Stephen this also means relinquishing control over his own destiny as he "is caught in a dream of origin which can never be realised. There is no outline beginning, there is only the desire for it, for a total independence from all and everyone else." (*Joyce* 48). Troublingly from this perspective, Stephen will never have the opportunity to have complete control over his past, and by this logic, the control to define his identity separately from history.

Furthermore, it is worth visiting Gibbons once more, for his contrast of Irish and American notions of space with specific reference in his analysis of the position of history in the Irish consciousness:

> The western genre is a hymn to the wilderness, and exercise pre-eminently of the spatial imagination which finds its images of freedom in the open expanses of the supposedly uninhabited great plains. Its Irish equivalent, however, looks for its authenticating images in time, extending its horizons through the accretions of history which acknowledge rather than deny, the pre-colonial presence of the landscape. (*Transformations* 13)

To elaborate, Gibbons' idea is that the landscape of Ireland provides for a continual reminder of colonisation, and that furthermore, Irish identity exists in the notions of history and colonisation in a comparative way to the American consciousness and its identification with possibility, expansion and freedom. The contrast between these outlooks, no matter how general, demonstrates the long-term damage of the colonial mindset that can henceforth also be read as affecting Stephen.

Stephen appears to place history in the same pantheon of colonialism, religion and nationalism. Accounting for this focus on history, Deane notes that Joyce "analyses the psychology of subjection in his people by showing the paralysis which has overtaken them in their endless, futile quest for an origin which will provide them with an identity securely their own" ("Joyce" 49). Thinking of this point retrospectively, the characters of *Dubliners* and the peripheral characters of *A Portrait* and *Stephen Hero* can all be observed to be searching for the right to independence, often without the ability to articulate the problem. Although Stephen has struggled with the same crisis, it seemed that in his recognition of the source of these identity problems, he had resolved this predicament. Yet this notion of history persists, as a counterpoint to Stephen, demonstrating that desire and articulation are not sufficient, that, to finally be free of the colonialism and nationalism that have been found to hold a constrictive hold over Irish identity, the individual must also make amends with history, and allow for the future inclusion of an identity that will never become attached to personal or national notions of the past.

History, like the other identity markers, is inclusive of a large section of the population and it would be just as daunting a task to dispel Irish history, as it would be to dispel colonialism, religion or nationalism. With this added difficulty, Stephen struggles to regain his previous confidence to engage with the task of addressing Irish identity. Therefore, reconsidering the argument from the onset of this thesis, it may be that history as understood in the postcolonial sense is the problem that prevents Stephen from articulation of an independent position. Because Stephen cannot find himself, or the person he wants to be, in the colonial history of Ireland, he becomes despondent, ultimately allowing the colonial power of history to define his nation and his personal identity.

Stephen's relatively extremist distrust of church, state, nationalism and now history, is addressed, when Buck attributes Stephen behaviour to the "cursed Jesuit strain in [him], only it's injected the wrong way" (8). This idea that Stephen has perverted the goals of his alma maters is again echoed by the whore, as Florry proclaims, "I'm sure you are a spoiled priest. Or a monk" (638). Stephen has rejected the majority identity but has failed to create an alternative response and instead is understood as something of a binary opposite to traditional Irish identity in the opinion of others. For Stephen, this is unfortunate as his early attempts at understanding Irish identity were clearly undertaken through a desire to help his nation, rather than to simply become the hateful, or mocking anti-Irishman that Buck and Florry here perceive. The significant shift here in the overall Joycean canon is that the development of Irish identity described in *Stephen Hero* and *Portrait* by Stephen cannot be accomplished by this character, but will instead be taken up by another.

Counterpoint to crisis: Leopold Bloom

Deane has pointed out that Joyce is "one of the few authors who legitimises the modern world, seeing its apparent "randomness and alienation as instances of an underlying diversity and communion" ("Joyce" 44). Indeed this positive perspective is embodied in Leopold Bloom. The future of Irish identity in the Joycean *oeuvre* has been passed to Bloom, who may be read as responding to Stephen's increasingly reactionary opposition to what was already a binary national mindset. Stephen has been observed in *Portrait* and *Stephen Hero* as closing off some options of Irish identity, such as his class biased judgements of Irish peasants and his gender biased considerations of women. In *Ulysses*, Stephen shows a lack of direction in his opposition to the Church, state and nationalist authorities that seek his conformity, all of which contributes to Stephen's identity deteriorating to binary reaction, or what appears to be blind opposition to the majority culture. Although Stephen's reaction to Irish identity therefore has not liberated Irish consciousness to structure itself freely, Stephen has valuably proposed the goal of liberating the national consciousness from the controlling apparatuses that must be forgone in order to create independently. In response to Stephen's frustration, *Ulysses* offers Bloom, who by way of his otherness and flexible identity can liberate the Irish consciousness from constrictive and limited alternatives, by breaking the binary systems, and accepting points from various competing forces. Based on the previously studied characters, this might seem strange, however, Bloom seems to realise all of the faults and inconsistencies in the modernising of Ireland and he directs Ireland to embrace what will either be a forced diversity or accepted hybridity.

More so than previous sections, this aspect of my argument owes a particular debt to Cheng, whose *Joyce, Race and Empire* inspired this interpretation of *Ulysses*. However, the goal of this section, and this thesis, is to expand Cheng's reading of Bloom so as to incorporate the whole of Joyce's texts in demonstrating that, for Joyce, decolonisation was at the centre of all his novels which continued to be updated by new approaches to the problem of colonial identity. Therefore, this final section of textual analysis focuses on the ultimate direction that Joyce would proscribe for the future of Irish identity.

Bloom as "other"

Fanon notes that "Within the framework of colonial domination there is not and there will never be such phenomena as new cultural departures or changes in the national culture" (191). Perhaps with respect to this idea, *Ulysses* must offer an outsider to do the job of not only proposing a development for national culture, but in truly proposing advancement and diversity. Consider how Bloom's identity is more open to interpretation than previous characters as in Molly's explanation of some of Bloom's exclusion as being due to, "Poldy" being "not Irish enough" (885-886). Although Bloom is born in Ireland, and considers himself Irish, many of his fixed identity traits do not correspond to perceived or conditioned assumptions of Irishness dictated by the apparatuses of power in colonial Ireland. Cheng observes that, "As we have seen, nations tend to construct themselves as imagined communities with a national essence, character, and identity, resulting in a value-laden hierarchy that writes out or homogenizes non-conforming 'others'" (211). Cheng's argument, while true for the general idea of nation, is especially relevant for the colonial nation seeking identity. From this perspective, Bloom reads as a rare representative of an "other" identity that the characters of *Dubliners* searched for, namely something besides the typical identifiers of race, colour, and creed. Although Bloom is too often shunned for his differences, he shows the characters of *Ulysses* those aspects of culture already existing in Irish society that could be included in Irish identity, if only these non-traditional elements were valued.

In the opening of "Ithaca" the catechism based narration asks, "Did he find four separating forces between his temporary quest and him?" with the response being, "Name, age, race, creed" (792). It is in this distinction that Bloom and Stephen are clearly separated, even forcibly so, by four of the most basic factors that construct identity, and yet the understanding these characters can offer one another is extremely valuable. Cheng describes the importance of realising what Bloom can mean for Irish identity, "It is the tragedy of a unisonant, monologic perspective that it is blind to the pluralism, heterogeneity, and multivalence of perspectives available – even within one's own nation" (197). Cheng's argument demonstrates the irony that when we feel united to our nation, we are in fact connecting to a vision of the nation similar to ourselves. In the case of the Ireland that Joyce describes, this limited definition therefore entails an Ireland identifying with the enforced visions of Irish identity promoted by nationalism, colonialism, and religion rather than a many-faced, cultural, ethnically and religiously pluralist vision that would perhaps be united by common goals rather than predetermined definitions.

Bloom's otherness creates a different perspective from which to interpret the majority culture and identity, as well as offering criticism that would perhaps be difficult for the majority population to articulate, a point comically made during Bloom's thoughts upon attending the Catholic burial ceremony of Paddy Dignam. However, even in the seemingly innocent air of much of Bloom's musings masks his ability to highlight problems of Irish identity that few characters realise. Kiberd comments on this issue as follow: "The implication is that those on the periphery see[ing] more of a situation than those centrally involved in it; and so Bloom, though ignorant of Catholic ritual, appears to take it more seriously than many who are fully familiar with it" (982). For instance, Bloom recognises the similarities in Catholic and Protestant religions, and even joins Irish and British nationalism with his once-off comment of the priest who has a tone of muscular Christianity about him (130). In making this connection, Bloom shows his awareness of these opposing traditions, but being free of them, is able to form his opinion without the associated values that would be assumed for someone who is included in one of these identity groups. Cheng notes that "Bloom is able to hold simultaneous perspectives, to imagine being other and thus to transcend the monologic narrowness of a single, cycloptic perspective" (177). Cheng's comment relates most easily to the "Cyclops" episode where Bloom tries in to expose the Citizen and his close-mined nationalism to alternative perspectives. The narrator attests to Bloom's ability to think beyond his own identity when he is reported as arguing, *"but don't you see? And but on the other hand"* (395). [13] Even for this isolated occasion, Bloom demonstrates his capacity to sympathise with the other. This brief instance of

---

[13] Joyce's italics

Bloom's multi-layered thinking ability is immediately contrasted as the narrator then returns his attention to the argument before him where Bloom protests in an attempt to be understood by the Citizen, "You don't grasp my point" to which the response, "Sinn Fein! Says the Citizen. Sinn Fein Amhain! The friends we love are by our side and the foes we hate before us" (395-396). The Citizen's comments embody the xenophobic binary thinking which Joyce has shown as permeating Irish identity.

Returning to Bloom's ability to see the problem of the Citizen's errors, Cheng comments on how those living on the fringe of the nation can see how absurd the idea of nationality as essential to one's essence. National identity is not something "eternal and natural" (196-197). Perhaps this knowledge of the irrationality of essential identities is what ironically allows Bloom to let his lawyer, J. J. O'Molloy, construct a racially motivated defence for Bloom's past crimes:

> My client is an infant of a poor foreign immigrant who started scratch as a stowaway and is now trying to turn an honest penny. The trumped up misdemeanour was due to a momentary aberration of heredity, brought on by hallucination, such familiarities as the alleged guilty occurrence being quite permitted in my client's native place, the land of the Pharaoh. (588-589)

This passage attributes Bloom's problems to his national and ethnic identities, which corresponds to Cheng's notion that to make anything a crime, attributable to nationality or identity, is absurd.

Bloom wants to understand the majority perspective, to see the alternative side to all situations and arguments, which is important for developing a more inclusive overall perspective. Kiberd make this point in his notes: "All through the day Bloom displays an admirable and rare capacity to see the world through the eyes and mind of others [. . .]" (introduction liii), which is the best way to get a grasp of the 'other' and therefore one's own culture as well. Consider, for example, the time Blooms spends trying to imagine life without sight, after his chance encounter with the blind man. Perhaps even more telling is Bloom's choice of reading for Molly, with knowledge of the affair, he considers something more vindictively titled *Fair Tyrants*, but ultimately chooses *The Sweets of Sin*, a novel that seems to glamorise a wife's adulterous affair. This gift comes with an unspoken acceptance or at least understanding of Molly's affair. Bloom, somewhat perversely, even seems to admire Molly's position to the extent that he becomes excited by the prose of this erotic novel.

Like the characters of *Dubliners*, Bloom is inclined to let his thoughts drift into fantasy, however in contrast to those prior characters, he prevents the fantasy from disrupting reality. The scene initially inspires the typical romantic associations with the other, as he considers the sensation of the produce and then visualises Turkey as

> [s]omewhere in the east: early morning: set off at dawn. Travel round in front of the sun, steal a day's march on him. Keep it up for ever never grow a day older technically. Walk along a strand, strange land, come to a city gate, sentry there, old ranker too, old Tweedy's big moustaches leaning on a long kind of a spear. Wander through awned streets. Turbaned faces going by. Dark caves of carpet shops, big man, Turko the terrible, seated crosslegged smoking a coiled pipe. Cries of sellers in the streets. Drink water scented with fennel sherbet. Dander

along all day. Might meet a robber or two. Well, meet him. Getting on to sundown. The shadows of the mosques along the pillars: priest with a scroll rolled up. A shiver of the trees, signal, the evening wind. I pass on. Fading gold sky. A mother watches me from her doorway. She calls her children home in their dark language. High wall: beyond strings twanged. Night sky, moon, violet, colour of Molly's new garters. Strings. Listen. A girl playing one of these instruments what do you call them: dulcimers. (68)

This extended passage actually reads like the fantasies of *Dubliners*, specifically those of "Araby." Consider Cheng's interpretation of "Araby" as a partial and constructed vision of what the other culture is like, which is disappointed when the narrator finds that the binary system of othering is unfounded, as the Araby fair does not represent his stereotypical vision of Oriental exoticness.[14] The narrator is defeated because the exoticness that he seeks in Ireland cannot be found at the fair, or anywhere else, as the his limited exposure to other cultures has distorted his understanding of national and cultural identity. With this danger in mind, Bloom attributes these Oriental stereotypes of the other culture and not to his real experience. However, just after concluding this vision, Bloom adds, "Probably not a bit like it really. Kind of stuff you read: in the track of the sun" (68). Consider how Bloom's comment corresponds to the boy's account from the opening of 'Araby', in which the boy summariwes the adventure novels that would perhaps encourage the stereotypical idealizations of foreign locations and cultures.

---

[14] Cheng's interpretation can be found in *Joyce, Race and Empire* (93-98).

Bloom's aversion to misleading fantasies is further illustrated when he briefly considers acting on a Turkish planting scheme and pictures the romantic vision: "Crates lined up on the quayside at Jaffa, chap ticking them off in a book, navvies handling them in soiled dungarees" (73). But again, this vision is quickly countered by a replacement of that stereotype with another, "No, not like that. A barren land, bare waste". Bloom goes on in a more pessimistic tone than perhaps anywhere else in the novel as he describes the desolation of the area's geography and history. Finally, in awareness of his previous morbidity, Bloom retracts "Well, I am here now. Morning mouth bad images. Got up wrong side of the bed" (73). Bloom here is aware of his generalizations in both cases, counterbalancing the overly positive views of the other like the narrator of 'Araby', and the negativity of the Citizen's view of the other, by discounting both visions as products of cultural stereotypes.

Essentially, Bloom has fantasies like other Joycean characters, but Bloom does not fantasise to escape reality. In "Circe," Bloom leaves the nymph and his hallucinatory fantasy as he realises, "But if there were only ethereal where would you be, postulants and novices" (661)? Bloom here realises the danger of living inside the fantasy rather than engaging with reality, and after this moment, Bloom may be observed taking a far more concrete interest in Stephen and his actually surroundings. Because Bloom accepts stereotypes for what they are, he is able to understand his own situation more clearly, and therefore his real interaction with others is largely positive, as is exampled by his admitted attraction to the otherness that blacks, nuns and women with glasses have for him (479). All of which serve to demonstrate Bloom's ability to understand himself as well as the other.

Flexible identity

To fully accept a flexible identity, Bloom must allow no single aspect of his identity to stay unchanging, including his gender identity. Nowhere can Bloom's ability to incorporate the feminine side of his personality be better seen than in the hallucinations of "Circe" where Dr Dixon proclaims Bloom's bill of health that he, "is a finished example of the new womanly man." This point may have been demonstrated by the sympathy and understanding Bloom has shown towards women throughout the day, but the extravagant nature of this chapter allows for the metaphor to continue into reality as the doctor announces, "He is about to have a baby." Bloom collaborates with this sentiment by proclaiming, "O, I so want to be a mother" (614). Contrast this outward show of extreme femininity with an earlier aggressive male fantasy. Bloom becomes distracted while in conversation with McCoy, when he notices a rich woman outside the Grosvenor Hotel. After considering her position and admiring her attire, Bloom harshly characterises her: "Like that haughty creature at the polo match. Women all for caste till you touch the spot. Handsome is and handsome does. Reserved about to yield. The honourable Mrs and Brutus is an honourable man. Possess her once take the starch out of her" (89).

Other examples of hyper-masculinity abound and contrast to Bloom's previously detailed femininity, but the erotic gaze and sexual objectification of Cissy Caffrey should also be considered. However, these instances of hyper-masculinity and femininity in turn are but examples of Bloom's ability to move from one end of the spectrum to the other. Bloom's ability to relate to or even become the opposite sex, while also simultaneously allowing him to foster a hyper-masculinity, establishes a case for the positive aspects of an identity that has the ability to understand both perspectives. Kiberd reads Bloom's gender identity inconsistencies as a national allegory:

> In espousing the ideal of androgyny, just one year after the declaration of the Irish Free State, *Ulysses* proclaimed itself a central text of national liberation. Against the either/or antithesis of British imperial psychology it demonstrated the superior validity of a both/and philosophy.
> (Introduction lxiv-lxvi)

The postcolonial Irish could do most by deconstructing the binary colonial definitions, rather than become a part of it. Kiberd's point is that Bloom's intentional sexuality ambiguity serves as a foil to the rigid identity of nationalist and colonialist philosophy, it is therefore by not advocating a fixed sense of sexuality that Bloom allows for a more inclusive and autonomously created alternative definition. In national terms, if Irish identity were to approach somewhat closer to Bloom's multiple perspective, then the nation would be able to accept the aspects of its society and culture that have been excluded by restrictive definitions of Irishness. This multi-inclusive identity also have a progressive ability to incorporate future foreign elements into Irish culture, unlike the identity of nationalism and colonialism that remain statically unaccepting of change.

Bloom effectively dismisses the inclusion that nationalist identity can offer because he realises that Irish nationalism is not a productive force beyond its initial and limited objective. Bloom's liberation from nationalism metaphorically adds to the overall Joycean contention that nationalism is merely a tool for political and ideological independence, but actually stifles a consciousness that seeks the autonomy to create a political and ideological philosophy. Kiberd makes this point in his description of the "Cyclops" episode:

> Bloom, as internationalist and socialist, profoundly stretches the Citizen's tolerance, enabling Joyce to do two things-to distinguish the former's liberation from the latter's nationalism, and then to show how closely Irish nationalist ideas are based on the English model which they claim to contest. (Introduction 1057)

Kiberd first points to Bloom's ability to think beyond the exclusionary nationalism that the Citizen promotes and adds that Bloom has avoided the trappings of nationalism, because of his awareness of the limitations of nationalism in general. This awareness of Bloom's can be observed in his consideration of the nationalist songs and atmosphere in "Sirens": "Ireland comes now. My country above the king, She listens. Who fears to speak of nineteen four? Time to be shoving" (368). Perhaps in annoyance at having heard this rhetoric too many times before, Bloom reiterates the catch phrases and is disappointed to see the barmaids, whom he has spent much of the chapter admiring, take an interest in this nationalistically encrypted entertainment. The quote however is useful for demonstrating how significant Bloom's aversion to nationalism is, as he would rather leave the pub than be subjected to it. If this instance seems too subtle a justification for this hypothesis, consider Bloom's actions later in the chapter, when he mocks the stupidity of the protagonist from the "Croppy Boy" and then punctuates Robert Emmett's speech from the dock, one of the most important speeches in the Nationalist cannon, with, "Pprrpffrrppfff" (376). With little subtlety, Bloom audibly demonstrates his aversion to the nationalist rhetoric.

While the Citizen may unconsciously connect his vision of the future of Ireland with mirror the successes of Britain, Bloom realises the inaccuracies that abound for a nationalist with an espoused aversion to Empire. Consider this speech that the Citizen makes that outwardly detests the Empire, but yet includes echoes of admiration:

> The fellow that will never be slaves, with the only hereditary chamber on the face of God's earth and their land in the hands of a dozen gamehogs and cotton ball barons. That's the great empire they boast about of drudges and whipped serfs. – On which the sun never rises, says Joe. – And the tragedy of it is, says the citizen, they believe it. The unfortunate yahoos believe it. (427)

Ironically, it seems that the Citizen believes British nationalist myth too, as his comments reiterate some of his own expressed desires: to be free of colonisation, to boast of his nation's superiority, to inflict violence. Of course all of these ideas have been previously reflected in the Citizen's speeches. In response to the Citizen's baffling position Bloom asks, "isn't discipline the same everywhere? I mean wouldn't it be the same here if you put force against force?" (427). With an awareness of the Citizen's lack of logic, Bloom is able to again demonstrate the contradiction of applying the British system of colonial authority to Ireland. When Bloom is safely out of Barney Kiernan's, he is able to reflect on his encounter with nationalist xenophobia and comment, "Ought to go home and laugh at themselves. Always want to be swilling in company. Afraid to be alone like a child of two. Suppose he hit me. Look at it other way round. Not so bad then. Perhaps not to hurt he meant" (496). Bloom at once dismisses the seriousness of the nationalist position and self posturing, and yet also can forgive the Citizen's ignorant violence.

Bloom's counter argument to the Citizen can initially be read a reactive pacifism to his counterpart's aggression. This is most visibly demonstrated in "Cyclops" where Bloom espouses "moderation and botheration" (421). While the concept of moderation to balance the Citizen's extremism is fairly straightforward, the idea of botheration is quite unique. Not using the standard definition of this word, Bloom allows "botheration" not just to mean a state of annoyance, but the state of possessing both at once. This new definition is the very idea of pluralism that Bloom as a character so crucially relays, in a most ironic misinterpretation.

But Bloom has a more positive, although hallicinatorily and idealistic, vision for the future of Irish consciousness than that of which previous characters could offer. Consider his coronation speech that largely promotes peace, love and acceptance:

> I stand for the reform of municipal morals and the plain ten commandments. New worlds for the old. Union of all, Jew, Moslem and gentile. Three acres and a cow for all children of nature. Saloon motor hearses. Compulsory mannual labour for all. All parks open to the public day and night. Electric disscrubber. Tuberculosis, lunacy, war and mendicancy must now cease. General amnesty, weekly carnival, with masked licence, bonuses for all, Esperanto the universal brotherhood. No more patriotism of barspongers and dropscial imposturs. Free money, free love and fee lay church in a free lay state. (611)

Alongside some of the more nonsensical comments, Bloom's address promotes a more inclusive identity, espousing general moral principles like the commandments and all religious affiliations, while disavowing the Church structure; bypassing any language questions by forwarding Esperanto and choosing a humanitarian respect for humanity in general rather than the exclusions of patriotism. It is perhaps worth mentioning that these ideas of inclusiveness continue as Bloom promotes, "Mixed races and mixed marriage" (611), further adding to the ideas of plurality and identities that allow for hybridity and change. Perhaps even more significant than the above rant about pluralism and diversity is Bloom's more conventional plea to Stephen on the case of the future of the nation and its identity:

> Of course, Mr Bloom proceeded to stipulate, you must look at both sides of the question. It is hard to lay down any hard and fast rules as to right and wrong but room for improvement all round there certainly is through every country, they say, our own distressful included, has the government it deserves. But with a little goodwill all round. It's all very fine to boast of muted superiority but what about muted equality? I resent violence or intolerance in any shape or form. It never reaches anything or stops anything. A revolution must come on the due instalments plan. It's a patent absurdity on the face of it to hate people because they live round the corner and speak another vernacular, so to speak. (745)

Bloom here demonstrates his philosophy of moderation, by not rushing to any quick decision and botheration, in the sense that equality of nations could be desired rather than supremacy. Furthermore, Bloom discusses the idea of revolution coming in pieces, which may be found to correspond with the overall Joycean oeuvre that deals with identity in a sort of instalment plan, novel by novel.

Bloom's personality is able to change and adapt, and therefore he is never in the position of having to define himself by outside powers such as colonialism or nationalism. It may be useful here to look at some instances of Bloom's flexibility of identity and consider the national metaphor that could be developed. Kiberd draws attention to this possibility in stating, "The alternative to fetishizing Cuchulainn and his warrior band was the courageous admission that there was no such thing as an Irish identity, ready-made and fixed, to be carried as a passport to eternity" (introduction lxxiv). Kiberd here is referencing the efforts of creating a national consciousness based on a shared history, ethnicity or religion, that Joyce's contemporaries attempted to varying degrees. By trying to make any of these created visions of Irishness authentic, Kiberd illustrates the central problem of identity that Joyce responds by creating a character who has the ability to change. Kiberd continues, "It makes the liberating concession that a person, or a nation has a plurality of identities, constantly remaking themselves as a result of perpetual renewals" (introduction lxxvii). Again, by having the opportunity to redefine his own identity and by avoiding the authorities that seek to prevent identity from revolution, Bloom metaphorically shows the nation the value of this freedom and his inclusive perspective.

In terms of Bloom's consideration of flexibility, his musing that "Silly fish learn nothing in a thousand years" (222) is worth noting, as it suggests that by refusing to change, the proverbial fish continues to be caught by the same hook. Similar to this metaphor for the pitfalls of fixedness, it is possible to compare Bloom's avoidance of fixed identity. For instance consider the ease with which Bloom changes his name: "I, Rudolph Virag, now resident at no 52 Chanbrassil Street, Dublin, formerly of Sxombatherly in the Kingdom of Hungary, hereby give notice that I have assumed and intend henceforth upon all occasions and at all times to be known by the name of Rudolph Bloom" (852). The remembered statement first demonstrates Bloom's ability to adopt a new place, name and therefore identity, while it also serves as a retrospective irony, as throughout the novel, Bloom has been know by many other names.

Bloom considers change as he ponders, "I was happier then. Or was that I? Or am I now? [. . .] can't bring back time [. . .] Useless to go back" (213-214). Initially Bloom considers how his identity has changed since Rudy's death and his marriage began to dissipate. Fortunately, Bloom does have a forward perspective in choosing to embrace the differences that change has brought, rather than vainly seek to regain a past identity that is already obsolete. In fact, Bloom's vision of the future is largely positive, despite the obvious failures of his marriage, particularly on this day. But he still considers the possibility of total reconciliation: "No son. Rudy. Too late now. Or if not? If not? If still" (367)? There continues to be a possibility of change even at this late moment for the marriage. Further still, consider Bloom's general philosophy, which so clearly supports this thesis, of "Forgive, forget, kismet" (594). This outlook comprises the ideas of peace, of detachment from history and also a positive acceptance of the future and past.

In a final thought about Bloom's character, Kiberd worries, "How can we hope to know Bloom when – to judge by the evidence presented here – he doesn't seem to know himself" (1124)? Kiberd indicates that if Bloom's identity is never fixed, then perhaps the problem is that Bloom does not truly understand himself. Indeed Kiberd is not the first to voice such criticism of Bloom's plural lives as Mrs Beaufoy charges, "Why, look at the man's private life! Leading a quadruple existence" (586)! The response to

Kiberd and Beaufoy must be that perhaps we cannot ever make a definitive assessment of someone's identity because identity and its characteristics are intended to be dynamic. It may be best to leave the final assessment of Bloom to Molly, who has proclaimed, "As well him as another" (933). This passage reveals that Bloom is intended as an opportunity for demonstrating the necessity of opening Irish identity beyond finite constructs, and that Bloom is not to be taken as an example or messiah for Irish identity. Molly's point is that Bloom's story is not special because he is Jewish, European, urban, middle-class, apolitical or any of the other possible identifiers. Bloom is most important because he is one representation of difference in a culture starved for plurality and flexibility.

Conclusion
Irish Identity After Bloom

Of course the Joycean oeuvre does not end with *Ulysses*, but it would be overly ambitious and not particularly productive for this study to analyse *Finnegans Wake* in the same manner as the previous texts. It is true that the *Wake* may represent an even a further stride towards a multiculturalism and decentralization of Irish identity as Emer Nolan and David Spurr have argued. Spurr encapsulates the postcolonial reading of *Finnegans Wake* in stating:

> To read Joyce as a decolonized writer is to recognize that his historical perspective on the final stages of the imperial era coincides with his creation of a text that calls into question, formally and thematically the structures of power from which writing is inherited. (119)

Indeed, The *Wake* may be the implementation of the plurality and multiculturalism developed in Bloom. But while the *Wake may* be this continuation, it is difficult to even classify as a novel. In trying to describe the unique experience of engaging Joyce's final work, Attridge notes that no one reads the Wake like a piece of literature. He suggests that if one wanted to really understand the *Wake*, one might want to learn about all cultures and histories:

> Far from demanding exhaustive knowledge, it can be seen as offering every reader, from every background, some familiar ground to walk on, precisely because it incorporates so much of the world's linguistic, cultural and historical knowledge. (*Cambridge Companion* 10)

While the objective of this thesis is not to extend the argument to the Wake specifically, Attridge and Spurr make points that tie Joyce's final work into exactly what has been the aim of this study: namely to show how Joyce's texts develop in their approach to the problems of colonial Irish identity. Yet I hesitate to continue because although a study of the *Wake* would address the plurality of identity, the blending of cultures, the breakdown of language, and the message of unity that the incredibly dense and fractured *Wake* ironically promotes, such a reading would also be grossly oversimplifying a work that has yet to, and may never be fully understood. For example Spurr quite correctly states, "the play of language breaks free from the formations of authority that-in the empire of letters-prescribe meaning in terms of narrative, syntactical logic, intelligibility and so on" (120). The generalities do seem to say that there is something very postcolonial about the idea behind the structure of *Finnegans Wake*, but detailed analysis of the text results in either sweeping overviews of the idea of the novel or close readings of a particular word pun.

Maybe my work will inspire the *Wake* to be reinvestigated from the perspective of national identity, but I do not believe that national identity would open the text to any new levels of understanding that have not already been explored. Nor do I believe that additional close reading in the same context that I have read the previous novels would result in progress towards understanding the *Wake*. In sum, I am confident of my text based close readings of *Dubliners* through *Ulysses*, where I can offer evidence for my opinions, whereas with the *Wake*, I feel even close reading of specifically charged passages would only provide anecdotal support of this study.

This thesis examined postcolonial theory for its value in studying the articulation of national identity. The postcolonial writer understands that the national culture cannot ignore the shock of colonisation; therefore the nation must adopt a hybrid identity if it is to realistically embrace the challenges of modernisation. It was also noted that Ireland and Joyce are often unwisely overlooked in the field of postcolonial theory. Although Ireland is unusual, it nevertheless should be regarded as a postcolonial nation because of its history.

After outlining the theoretical perspective of this study, the argument progresses to a close reading of the texts, beginning with *Dubliners*. In Joyce's collection of short stories, the reader finds characters who want escape and freedom, but rather than try to create these aspirations in reality, they hide in fantasy and in self delusion. Furthermore, when these characters were not content with escapism, they tried to mimic the coloniser and reap the benefits of exploitation. In this first encounter with Joyce's writing, colonialism and its destructive effects on national culture, self-esteem and the general well being of the nation are observed. However, the collection does little in way of offering a solution, as nationalism and patriotic culture are either dismissed or occluded.

Joyce's treatment of colonialism develops significantly when we are introduced to Stephen Dedalus in *A Portrait of the Artist as a Young Man* and *Stephen Hero*. In these texts the protagonist struggles with his personal development and with his realization that the imperialist forces of British colonialism and Roman Catholicism control Ireland. While the British rule Irish law, government and culture, the Roman Catholic religion dictates Irish morality and politics. Stephen's *Bildungsroman* also applies to the nation that must develop apart from these constrictive forces that seek to dictate Irish identity and do not allow the Irish to autonomously create themselves.

Despite Stephen Dedalus's advancements, Joyce continues to focus his attention on the question of Irish identity, and ultimately leaves its articulation and freedom to Leopold Bloom, who offers a vision of Ireland that is inclusive and forward-looking, postnationalist and modern without giving a definitive right to any group or person to control 'Irishness'. Perhaps in reaction to the fear of a nation that does not have fixed identity, recent scholarship on 'Irishness' has speculated on the open question of Irish national identity: "The endless revelation of an absence at the heart of modern Irish identity must surely become frustrating when it comes to the question haunting every critical discourse: what is to be done?" (Graham and Kirkland, *Ireland* 45).

As Graham and Kirkland note, Irish identity in modern Ireland is undefined, but that is because everything is changing. With the influence of new forms of cultural imperialism from the United States of America and Europe, along with a greater influx of immigrants from the European Union and the asylum seekers, Ireland is growing closer to Joyce's vision of an open island. Deane's comments in regards to Finnegans Wake are true also of Irish modernity: "If Ireland could not be herself, then, by way of compensation, the world would become Ireland. Thus is the problem of Irish identity solved" ("Joyce" 53). While perhaps not the entire world has been brought to Ireland in a Wakeian sense, still, Ireland, as this thesis has argued, can realistically only become more diverse by accepting the changes that have occurred and will occur in national culture.

In making reference to the collaboration of black cultures around the world Fanon writes: "The 'black world' will see the light and from Ghana, Birago Diop from Senegal, Hampate Ba from the Sudan and Saint-Clair Drake from Chicago will not hesitate to assert the existence of common ties and a motive power that is identical" (Fanon 171).

Consider the irony of Fanon's desire to bring the black cultures of the world together in light of the humour of Roddy Doyle's character, Jimmy Rabitte, who comments that "[t]he Irish are the niggers of Europe, lads" (9). Skin colour aside, Ireland continues to represent itself as an other among the former colonisers of Europe. The point being that Ireland shares a colonial past with the traditionally accepted postcolonial nations as well as the colonisers. I hope the future of postcolonial studies will not reside in comparisons of national literature and evaluations of "postcolonialness," but there is something to be gained in promoting the dialogue between cultures. Perhaps Joyce's concept of Irishness will contribute to an anti-nationalistic idea of literature, expending our reading of national literatures in the widest possible scope, beyond the fixed concepts of nation and nationality, making us aware of the interconnectedness of humanity.

Bibliography

Althusser, Louis. *Lenin and Philosophy and Other Essays.* Trans. Ben Brewster. London: Unwin, Gresham, 1971.

Anderson, Benedict. *Imagined Communities: Reflections on the Origin and Spread of Nationalism.* Revised and expanded edition. London: Verso, 1991.

Ashcroft, Bill, Gareth Griffiths, and Helen Tiffin. *The Empire Writes Back: Theory and Practice in Postcolonial Literatures.* London: Routledge, 1989.

___, eds. *The Post-Colonial Studies Reader.* London and New York: Routledge, 1995.

Attridge, Derek, ed. *The Cambridge Companion to James Joyce.* Cambridge: Cambridge University Press, 1990.

___. *Joyce Effects: On Language, Theory and History.* Cambridge: Cambridge University Press, 2000.

___, Marjorie Howes, eds. *Semicolonial Joyce.* Cambridge: Cambridge University Press, 2000.

Bhabha, Homi K., ed. *Nation and Narration.* New York: Routledge, 1990.

Brown, Terence. Introduction and appendices. *Dubliners.* New York: Penguin, 1992. xii-xlviv, 227-317.

___. "New Literary Histories." *Irish Historical Studies* 30.119 (1997): 462-470.

Cairns, David, and Shaun Richards. *Writing Ireland: Colonialism, Nationalism and Culture.* Manchester: Manchester University Press, 1988.

Castle, Gregory, ed. *Postcolonial Discourses: An Anthology.* Malden, Massachusetts: Blackwell, 2001.

Chakrabarty, Dipesh. "Minority Histories, Subaltern Pasts." *Postcolonial Studies* 1.1 (1998): 15-29.

Cheng, Vincent J. *Joyce, Race and Empire*. Cambridge: Cambridge University Press, 1995.
Clowley, Ethal, and Jim MacLaughlin, eds. *Under the Belly of the Tiger: Class, Race, Identity and Culture in the Global Ireland*. Dublin: Irish Reporter Publications, 1997.
Deane, Seamus, ed. *The Field Day Anthology of Irish Writing*. Derry: Field Day Publications, 1991.
___. Introduction and notes. Joyce, *Portrait* vii-xlvii, 277-329.
___. "Joyce the Irishman." Attridge, *Cambridge Companion* 31-53.
___. *Nationalism, Colonialism, and Literature*. Minneapolis: Minnesota, 1990.
___. *Strange Country: Modernity and Nationhood in Irish Writing Since 1790*. Oxford: Claredon, 1997.
Doyle, Roddy. *The Commitments*. London: Vintage, 1998.
Drabble, Margaret, ed. *The Oxford Companion to English Literature*. Sixth edition. Oxford: Oxford University Press, 2001.
Eagleton, Terry. *Heathcliff and the Great Hunger: Studies in Irish Culture*. London: Verso, 1995.
Ellmann, Richard. *James Joyce*. New York: Oxford University Press, 1959.
Fairhall, James. *James Joyce and the Question of Nationalism*. Cambridge: Cambridge University Press, 1993.
Fanon, Frantz. *The Wretched of the Earth*. Trans. Constance Farrington. Pref. Jean-Paul Sartre. London: Penguin, 2001.
Foster, Roy. *The Irish Story: Telling Tales and Making It up in Ireland*. London: Penguin, 2001.
Gibbons, Luke. *Transformations in Irish Culture*. Cork: Cork University Press in association with Field Day, 1996.
___. "Where Wolfe Tone's Statue Was Not: Joyce, Monuments and Memory." McBride, *History* 139-159.

Graham, Colin, and Willy Maley. "Irish Studies and Postcolonial Theory." Introduction. *Irish Studies Review* 7.2 (1999): 149-152.

___, and Richard Kirkland, eds. *Ireland and Cultural Theory: The Mechanics of Authenticity*. London: Macmillan, 1999.

Halloran, Thomas. "Articulating Colonial Irish Identity in *Dubliners*: Homogeneity as Productive of Fantasy." *In-Between: Essays & Studies in Literary Criticism* 12 (2003): 217-227.

___. "Joyce and Postcolonial Literature: Creating an Inclusive Irish Identity." *New Voices in Irish Criticism 5*. Ed. Anne Coughlan . Dublin: Four Courts, 2005. 187-197.

Harkness, David. 1999. "Ireland." *Historiography*. Ed. Robin Winks. Vol. 5. of *The Oxford History of the British Empire*. Oxford: Oxford University Press, 1999. 114-133.

Heaney, Seamus. "Crediting Poetry: The Nobel Lecture 1995." *Open Ground Poems, 1966-1996*. London: Faber and Faber, 1998. 445-467.

"History." *Oxford English Dictionary Online*. Oxford University Press. 6 Dec. 2001 <http://dictionary.oed.com>.

Hobsbawn, E. J. *Nations and Nationalism since 1780: Programme, Myth, Reality*. Second edition. Cambridge: Cambridge University Press, 1992.

Hofheinz, Thomas C. *Joyce and the Invention of Irish History*. Cambridge: Cambridge University Press, 1995.

Howe, Stephen. *Ireland and Empire: Colonial Legacies in Irish History and Culture*. Oxford: Oxford University Press, 2000.

Hyde, Douglas. "The Necessity for De-Anglicizing Ireland." *Language, Lore and Lyrics: Essays and Lectures*. By Hyde. Dublin: Irish Academic Press, 1986. 153-170.

Jameson, Fredric. *Nationalism, Colonialism and Literature: Modernism and Imperialism*. A Field Day Pamphlet 14. Derry: Field Day Theatre Company, 1988.

Jeffares, Norman A., and Brendan Kennelly, eds. *Joycechoyce: The Poems in Verse and Prose of James Joyce*. Schull: Robert Rinehart, 1992.

Jeffery, Keith. 1996. *An Irish Empire: Aspects of Ireland and the British Empire*. Manchester: Manchester University Press.

Joyce, James. "After the Race." Joyce, *Dubliners* 35-42.

___. "Counterparts." Joyce, *Dubliners* 82-94.

___. "The Dead." Joyce, *Dubliners* 175-226.

___. *Dubliners*. New York: Penguin, 1993.

___. "An Encounter." Joyce, *Dubliners* 11-20.

___. "Gas from a Burner." *The Critical Writings of James Joyce*. Ed. Ellsworth Mason and Richard Ellmann. New York: Viking, 1959.

___. *Occasional, Critical and Political Writing*. Ed. Kevin Barry. Oxford: Oxford University Press, 2000.

___. *A Portrait of the Artist as a Young Man*. New York: Penguin, 1993.

___. *Stephen Hero*. Frogmore: Triad/Panther1977.

___. "Two Gallants." Joyce, *Dubliners* 43-55.

___. *Ulysses: Annotated Student's Edition*. London: Penguin, 1992.

Kennedy, Dane. "Imperial History and Post-Colonial Theory." *Journal of Imperial and Commonwealth History* 24.3 (1996): 345-363.

Kennedy, Liam. *Colonialism, Religion and Nationalism in Ireland*. Belfast: The Queen's University of Belfast, 1996.

Kiberd, Declan. Introduction and notes. *Ulysses: Annotated Student's Edition*. London: Penguin, 1992. ix-lxxxviv, 935-1195.

———. *Inventing Ireland: The Literature of a Modern Nation.* London: Vintage, 1996.
Lawrence, Karen R. ed. *Transcultural Joyce.* Cambridge: Cambridge University Press, 1998.
Leerssen, Joep. "Monuments and Trauma: Varieties of Remembrance." McBride 204-222.
———. *Remembrance and Imagination: Patterns in the Historical and Literary Representation of Ireland in the Nineteenth Century.* Cork: Cork University Press, 1996.
Livesay, James, and Stuart Murray. "Postcolonial Theory and Modern Irish Culture." *Irish Historical Studies* 30.119 (1997): 452-461.
Lloyd, David. *Anomalous States: Irish writing and the post-colonial movement.* Dublin: Lilliput, 1993.
———. *Ireland After History.* Cork: Cork University Press, 1999.
———. "Cultural Theory and Ireland." *Bullan: An Irish Studies Journal* 3.1(1997): 87-92.
Macaulay, Thomas. "Minute on Indian Education." Ed. Bill Gareth Griffiths and Helen Tiffin. *The Post-colonial Studies Reader.* New York: Routledge, 1995.
Mason, Ellsworth, and Richard Ellmann. eds. *The Critical Writing of James Joyce.* New York: Viking; 1959.
Mathews, P. J., ed. *New Voices in Irish Criticism.* Dublin: Four Courts, 2000.
McBride, Ian, ed. *History and Memory in Modern Ireland.* Cambridge: Cambridge University Press, 2001.
McClintock, Anne. "Angel of Progress: Pitfalls of the Term "Post-Colonialism." *Colonial Discourse and Post-Colonial Theory: A Reader.* Ed. Patrick Williams and Laura Chrisman. New York: Harvester Wheatsheaf, 1993.

McCarthy, Conor. *Modernisation, Crisis and Culture in Ireland, 1969-1992*. Dublin: Four Courts, 2000.

Mishra, Vijay, and Bob Hodge. "What is Post(-)colonialism?" *Colonial Discourse and Post-Colonial Theory: A Reader*. Ed. Patrick Williams and Laura Chrisman. New York: Harvester Wheatsheaf, 1993.

Ngũgĩ wa Thiong'o. *Decolonising the Mind: The Politics of Language in African Literature*. Nairobi: Heinemann Kenya, 1981.

Nolan, Emer. *James Joyce and Nationalism*. London and New York: Routledge, 1995.

O'Brien, Eugene. *The Question of Irish Identity in the Writing of William Butler Yeats and James Joyce*. Lewiston: Mellen, 1998.

O'Connor, Joseph. *The Secret World of the Irish Male*. Dublin: New Island, 1994.

Ó hEithir, Breandan. *A Pocket History of Ireland*. Dublin: O'Brien, 1996.

Potts, Willard. *Joyce and the Two Irelands*. Austin: University of Texas Press, 2000.

Rabate, Jean-Michel. *James Joyce and the Politics of Egoism*. Cambridge: Cambridge University Press, 2001.

Renan, Ernest. *The Poetry of the Celtic Races and Other Studies*. London: W. Scott, 1896.

Riquelme, John Paul. "Stephen Hero, and *A Portrait of the Artist as a Young Man*: Styles of Realism and Fantasy." Attridge, *Cambridge Companion* 103-130.

Robbins, Bruce. "The Newspapers Were Right: Cosmopolitanism, Forgetting and 'The Dead'" *Interventions: International Journal of Postcolonial Studies* 5.1 (2003): 101-112.

Said, Edward. *Culture and Imperialism*. London: Vintage, 1994.

___. *Nationalism, Colonialism and Literature: Yeats and Decolonization.* A Field Day pamphlet 15. Derry: Field Day Theatre Company, 1988.
___. *Orientalism.* London: Penguin, 1991.
Smyth, Gerry. "Irish Studies, Postcolonial Theory and the 'New' Essentialism.'" *Irish Studies Review* 7.2 (1999):149-152.
___. *The Novel and the Nation: Studies in the New Irish Fiction.* London, Chicago: Pluto, 1997.
___. *Space and the Irish Cultural Imagination.* Basingstoke: Palgrave, 2001.
Spivak, Gayatri Chakravorty. *In Other Worlds: Essays in Cultural Politics.* New York and London: Routledge, 1988.
Spurr, David. *Joyce and the Scene of Modernity.* James Joyce Series. Gainesville: University Press of Florida, 2002.
Stewart, Bruce. "Inside Nationalism: A Meditation upon Inventing Ireland." *Irish Studies Review* 6.1 (1998): 5-16.
Tomlinson, John. *Cultural Imperialism: A Critical Introduction.* London: Pinter, 1994.
Walder, Dennis. *Post-Colonial Literatures in English: History, Language and Theory.* Malden, Massachusetts: Blackwell, 1998.
Washbrook, D. A.. "Orients and Occidents: Colonial Discourse Theory and the Historiography of the British Empire." *Historiography.* Ed. Robin Winks. Vol. 5. of *The Oxford History of the British Empire.* Oxford: Oxford University Press, 1999. 596-611.
Willams, Patrick, and Laura Chrisman. *Colonial Discourse and Post-Colonial Theory: A Reader.* New York: Harvester Wheatsheaf, 1993.
___, Trevor L. *Reading Joyce Politically.* Gainesville: University Press of Florida, 1997.

Yeats, W. B. *The Collected Plays of W. B. Yeats*. London: Macmillan, 1952.

STUDIES IN ENGLISH LITERATURES

Edited by Koray Melikoğlu

ISSN 1614-4651

1. *Özden Sözalan*
   The Staged Encounter
   Contemporary Feminism and Women's Drama
   2nd, revised editon
   ISBN 3-89821-367-6

2. *Paul Fox (ed.)*
   Decadences
   Morality and Aesthetics in British Literature
   ISBN 3-89821-573-3

3. *Daniel M. Shea*
   James Joyce and the Mythology of Modernism
   ISBN 3-89821-574-1

4. *Paul Fox and Koray Melikoğlu (eds.)*
   Formal Investigations
   Aesthetic Style in Late-Victorian and Edwardian Detective Fiction
   ISBN 978-3-89821-593-0

5. *David Ellis*
   Writing Home
   Black Writing in Britain Since the War
   ISBN 978-3-89821-591-6

6. *Wei H. Kao*
   The Formation of an Irish Literary Canon in the Mid-Twentieth Century
   ISBN 978-3-89821-545-9

7. *Bianca Del Villano*
   Ghostly Alterities
   Spectrality and Contemporary Literatures in English
   ISBN 978-3-89821-714-9

8. *Melanie Ann Hanson*
   Decapitation and Disgorgement
   The Female Body's Text in Early Modern English Drama and Poetry
   ISBN 978-3-89821-605-5

9. *Shafquat Towheed (ed.)*
   New Readings in the Literature of British India, c.1780-1947
   ISBN 978-3-89821-673-9

10. *Paola Baseotto*
    "Disdeining life, desiring leaue to die"
    Spenser and the Psychology of Despair
    ISBN 978-3-89821-567-1

11. *Annie Gagiano*
    Dealing with Evils
    Essays on Writing from Africa
    ISBN 978-3-89821-867-2

12   Thomas F. Halloran
     James Joyce: Developing Irish Identity
     A Study of the Development of Postcolonial Irish Identity in the Novels of James Joyce
     ISBN 978-3-89821-571-8

FORTHCOMING (MANUSCRIPT WORKING TITLES)

Lance Weldy
Seeking a Felicitous Space
The Dialectics of Women and Frontier Space in *Giants in the Earth, Little House on the Prairie,* and *My Antonia*
ISBN 3-89821-535-0

Kevin Cole
Levity's Rainbow
Menippean Poetics in Swift, Fielding, and Sterne
ISBN 3-89821-654-3

Pablo Armellino
Obscene Spaces in Australian Narrative
ISBN 978-3-89821-873-3

Series Subscription

Please enter my subscription to the series **Studies in English Literatures**, ISSN 1614-4651, as follows:

- ❏ complete series   OR   ❏ English-language titles
-   ❏ German-language titles

starting with
- ❏ volume # 1
- ❏ volume # ___
  - ❏ please also include the following volumes: #___, ___, ___, ___, ___, ___,

- ❏ the next volume being published
  - ❏ please also include the following volumes: #___, ___, ___, ___, ___, ___,

- ❏ 1 copy per volume   OR   ❏ ___ copies per volume

Subscription within Germany:

You will receive every title on 1st publication at the regular bookseller's price incl. s & h and VAT.

Payment:
❏ Please bill me for every volume.
❏ Lastschriftverfahren: Ich/wir ermächtige(n) Sie hiermit widerruflich, den Rechnungsbetrag je Band von meinem/unserem folgendem Konto einzuziehen.

Kontoinhaber: _____ Kreditinstitut: _____
Kontonummer: _____ Bankleitzahl: _____

International Subscription:

Payment (incl. s & h and VAT) in advance for
- ❏ 10 volumes/copies (€ 319.80)   ❏ 20 volumes/copies (€ 599.80)
- ❏ 40 volumes/copies (€ 1,099.80)

Please send my books to:

NAME_____DEPARTMENT_____
ADDRESS _____
POST/ZIP CODE_____COUNTRY _____
TELEPHONE _____EMAIL_____

date/signature_____

Please fax to: **0511 / 262 2201 (+49 511 262 2201)**
or mail to: *ibidem*-Verlag, Julius-Leber-Weg 11, D-30457 Hannover, Germany
or send an e-mail: ibidem@ibidem-verlag.de

***ibidem*-**Verlag

Melchiorstr. 15

D-70439 Stuttgart

info@ibidem-verlag.de

www.ibidem-verlag.de
www.ibidem.eu
www.edition-noema.de
www.autorenbetreuung.de